BUILD A BUSINESS NOT A JOB

This publication is designed to provide accurate and authoritative information in regard to the subject matter covered. It is sold with the understanding that the publisher is not engaged in rendering legal, accounting, or other professional service. If legal advice or other expert assistance is required, the service of a competent professional person should be sought.

While the publisher and author have used their best efforts in preparing this book, they make no representations with respect to the accuracy or completeness of the contents of this book and specifically disclaim any implied warranties of merchantability or fitness for a particular purpose. Neither the publisher nor author shall be liable for any loss of profit or any other commercial damages, including but not limited to special, incidental, consequential, or other damages.

The following trademarks are the exclusive property of Maui Millionaires, LLC and are used with permission:

Self-Employment Trap™, Maui Millionaires®, and Level Three Business Audit™.

Maui Mastermind® and Level Three Map™ are exclusive trademarks of Maui Mastermind (NV), LLC and are used with permission.

ISBN:
Paperback: 978-1-958545-01-0
Hardcover: 978-1-958545-02-7

Printed in the United States of America

BUILD A BUSINESS NOT A JOB

Grow Your Business & Get Your Life Back

DAVID FINKEL

AND STEPHANIE HARKNESS

CONTENTS

FOREWORD

What a strange world it is that I'm here today contributing to this book designed to help business owners like you take your businesses to the next level. You see, I came to the world of business in the most unexpected way—through public education!

I was a home economics teacher in San Jose, California. I spent 13 years in public education, leaving it to start my first business, Expressions in Fine Jewelry. A gemologist friend and I created a high-end jewelry company serving personal clients. For six years, I flew around the world meeting our clients, sometimes carrying as much as $3 million worth of jewels in my briefcase. Exciting as that may seem, it got old after a while. The business needed me to be there at every step, every day, day after day. So when my husband Jack took early retirement from General Electric where he worked as a quality engineering manager, we made a decision that totally changed our lives. We chose to build a business together.

We looked around at various opportunities—from doing our own start-up, to buying a franchise, to purchasing an existing business. In the end, we opted to buy a small injection molding plastics manufacturing company near our home called Pacific Plastics and Engineering (today called JunoPacific).

I look back and think *what in the world were we doing?!* We didn't know anything about injection molded plastic manufacturing; we had never co-owned a manufacturing business before. In my heart, I still felt like a schoolteacher, for heaven's sake! But both Jack and I had a deep belief in each other, and we knew we didn't want to live our lives wondering *what if* …You've met those people, right? They spend the long days of their later years wondering and sighing *if only* …and *I wish we had…*

Well, we didn't want that to be us, so we stepped out into the unknown and invested $60,000—my entire retirement savings through my teacher's pension—to buy this company and go after our dreams.

I wish I could tell you it was all roses and champagne from there on, but it wasn't. Our first few months in business, we learned that all those customers the seller had told us about were less than happy with customer service. And the financial books he had shown us were more fiction than fact. Faced with these challenges, we did what most self-employed people do—we rolled up our sleeves and got to work. Jack took over the operations and began the painstaking process of mastering manufacturing injection molding plastics products. And I stepped into the role of running everything else—sales, marketing, financial management—as well as providing big-picture leadership of the business.

It took us three years of hard work, but we turned the business around. At that point, we needed to make a decision. Did we want it to continue as a mom-and-pop business that revolved around Jack and me, or did we want to step up and build a business that was bigger and more substantive than just the two of us? We decided to grow and scale the business.

Back then we didn't have the road map you have in this book. We didn't know how to build our core business infrastructure and systems. No one showed us the distinction of building not for control, but to establish intelligent business controls to empower the business, not just Jack and me as owners.

Still, over the following three years we managed to figure those things out and turn JunoPacific into a highly successful, high-end manufacturer that runs 24/7 in the United States and has operations in India. Over time we repositioned the company to be the go-to source to launch new projects in the laparoscopic medical device and biotech world. For the past few years Jack and I enjoyed the cash flow, satisfaction, and freedom of owning an "owner independent" company. We traveled the world, keeping in touch with the business to make sure it stayed on track, trusting the team, systems, and culture to guide and operate it day in, day out.

Then in 2011 we received an offer to purchase the company for more money than we could have imagined, and we accepted the offer, closing in the spring of 2011.

Why am I sharing all this with you? Because if I can do it, so can you. Just imagine: I was an ex-schoolteacher with no formal training in business who 25 years earlier had stepped out in faith with my husband and bought a small manufacturing business. With some painful trial and error we had grown the company into a dominant niche player. Now here we were, harvesting a high-eight-figure windfall from the sale of the company.

Looking back, I recognize that anyone can build an owner-independent business if they set their minds to it and follow the known steps to do so. What amazes me is how consistent the challenges are that face a business, regardless of industry, and that there are known solutions to the challenges you'll face. Creating a structure, accountability, and processes makes all the difference. Too many business owners make things harder for themselves by holding on to the belief that their business is different. Jack and I built systems and feedback to run a multimillion-dollar business that was truly independent of the two of us. Sure, we loved seeing results grow, but we took the known steps to develop our company. We groomed a solid, core leadership team that could run the business day in, day out. We made the company systems reliant, with strong processes and procedures that allowed it to produce exceptional value consistently for our customers and other stakeholders. And we developed a clear mission and culture that guided our company's operations, even when we were out of the country on extended vacations.

I first met David as a client of Maui Mastermind®, when in 2004 Jack and I attended the *Maui Mastermind Wealth Summit*. At $30,000 per couple, the *Wealth Summit* may be the most exclusive business owner retreat around. Over the next few years, I enjoyed participating in the event, gaining great insights and connecting with a wonderful peer group of ambitious yet caring business owners. When I was invited to become a Maui Advisor in 2007, I was honored. I had gained so much from the community that I loved sharing my experiences with other business owners who were working to grow their businesses and designing the lives they wanted.

Which brings me to this book. You're going to love it, by the way. It's like finding the secret treasure map that every business owner dreams of but rarely finds. In it you'll discover a clear, concrete map that will take you through the entire life cycle of your business from launch to exit.

This is the book I wish someone had handed to me 26 years ago when I started out in our own business. Not only would it have saved *me* from painful, costly mistakes, but it would have relieved so much of the doubt and uncertainty I felt because of all the conflicting advice I received over the years.

After being involved with a number of successful start-ups in Silicon Valley, including the growth of our manufacturing business, I can tell you from my perspective as a serial entrepreneur that this map and these distinctions are incredibly powerful. They work.

But it's up to you to put these ideas into practice—to invest the time and focused attention to follow this map and apply the concrete strategies to your business.

What's the payoff for all that effort? A multimillion-dollar owner-independent business that you love owning again.

It is possible for you—you just need to take the first step and apply what you learn in this book.

Stephanie Harkness
Pebble Beach, California

INTRODUCTION

Do you own your business, or does your business own you?

We know that's a blunt way to start a business book, but our experiences working with thousands of business owners have taught us that you appreciate candor and directness.

So have you built a business or a job for yourself? If you don't show up at the office tomorrow morning, will your business continue to thrive and grow, or will it grind to a halt? What about if you took an unexpected week off? A month? A quarter?

The facts weigh heavily against the average business owner. According to the U.S. Census Bureau, 88.6 percent of U.S.-based businesses still require the owner to be there as the primary person responsible for core functions like producing the product or service, managing the day-to-day operations, and managing the financial aspects of the business.

And according to the Wells Fargo/Gallup Small Business Index, the average small business owner works 52 hours a week, 57 percent of them work six days a week, and more than 20 percent work *seven* days a week. How do you know if this book is for you? If you're a seasoned business owner who wants to rapidly accelerate your company's growth, but to do it in a way that enables you to get your life back, this book is for you.

If the business you've built has become more of a chore, where you still show up every day because it supports you and your family, but the pressure and strain of everything on your shoulders, combined with the long hours, have worn away much of what you used to love about the business, then this book is for you.

If you crave time freedom and want your business to be strong enough to operate smoothly—independent of your daily attendance at the office—this book is for you.

If you want a proven model to scale your company that strengthens its independence from you, the owner, this book is for you.

If you have the courage to unflinchingly look at the true facts of what you've built and to take active steps to build an owner-independent company, this book is for you.

We understand what you're facing—we've faced the exact same thing in our business lives.

You feel trapped in the business. It's as if there just aren't enough hours in the day to get even a fraction of your to-do list done. You feel pulled in a thousand different directions with too many conflicting demands. You feel vulnerable to the loss of a key team member, fearing that if that were to happen you'd be in an even worse place than you are in today. And most of all, you feel overwhelmed with too much to do, not sure where to start, and with no clear plan in place.

Well, we've got good news for you. This book is your opportunity for things to be different. It marks the starting point for you to build a better, stronger, more profitable company.

Take the example of Mark and Diana Huha, owners of Quality Property Maintenance, a successful service business in San Diego, California, that contracts with large homeowner associations to care for and maintain their common areas. When David first met this couple in June 2012, they were burned out and ready to quit. They had been running their business for more than a decade, earning a comfortable living and raising their family. Their business worked, but only because of the long hours they put in to keep it working. In a typical week, Mark would work 40 to 50 hours in the field, supervising his maintenance teams, and then put in another 20 to 25 hours per week at night and on weekends trying to keep up with the billing, payroll, and administrative details of running the company.

In the coming chapters you'll learn precisely how Mark and Diana escaped this 70- to 75-hour-a-week trap, doubling their sales and cutting their work hours in half, and how you can too.

You'll also learn how Bruce, a skilled surgeon, tamed his medical practice not by working more, but rather by working less, and getting his medical practice to operate more smoothly and systematically.

And you'll meet Bonnie Hacker, owner of a successful service business, and learn how in six years she was able to not only grow her company by 145 percent to sales of $1,350,000 but at the same time to reduce her working hours to under 10 hours a month, effectively enjoying an owner-independent company.

You'll also meet Brian, a second-generation manufacturer who took over the family business after the death of his father. At the time, his company's operating profit was under 3 percent and the company was at risk of failing. Following the map laid out in this book, over a 48-month period, Brian's company quadrupled its operating profit while at the same time increasing its owner independence by 300 percent.

And you'll discover how Jennifer Lyle, the owner of a niche software company, escaped the self-employment trap and grew her company's market value tenfold over a six-year period, while at the same time gaining the ability to enjoy a greater sense of time freedom than she ever thought possible.

We want to be clear—we are primarily businesspeople, not authors. Between us, we've built over a dozen successful companies with a combined market value in the hundreds of millions of dollars. We have owned and scaled businesses in diverse areas, from manufacturing to service companies, real estate companies, professional services firms, retail businesses, and online companies. This book contains the guiding principles and the concrete formulas we've developed in the successful scaling of our companies. Essentially what this book gives you is a proven map that you can apply to consistently create the dual results of business growth *and* personal freedom.

Everything you read in this book has been tested and validated. Over the past decade David has taught this same methodology to build and scale an owner independent company to more than 100,000 business owners around the world, and the results his clients have enjoyed prove that the concepts, strategies, and tools contained in this book are transferrable and get results. When you follow the methodology we'll share in this book, not only do you get growth in sales and profits, but you'll also enjoy increased time freedom as the business owner. You'll get a company that is stable, vibrant, valuable, *and* a joy to own.

Whether your business is a small, five-person online seller doing $635,000 a year in sales, or a 12-person medical practice with annual revenue of $2.4 million, or a 26-person service business with annual sales of $7.5 million, or even a 345-person manufacturing company with $34 mil- lion a year in sales, this book will give you clear, actionable insights to grow your business and get your life back.

Still, there are going to be a few business owners who insist their business is different—that it's "special." Sure, they could imagine these ideas and this methodology working for *other* people's businesses, but not for theirs.

The manufacturer says, *"I can't do it but could see how this would work for a professional services firm."* The professional services firm says, *"We can't do it, but we can see how this would work for a blue-collar services company."* The blue-collar services business says, *"I can't do it, but I can see how this would work for an online company.*" The online company says, "*I can't do this, but I can see how a medical practice could use this road map.*" All the while, around them and under their very noses, thousands of businesses in their own industry quietly go about increasing their owner independence year after year. But still there are going to be a stubborn few business owners insisting on their companies' uniqueness, as if in the history of the world no business like theirs ever progressed past the "owner reliant" stage.

What they don't realize is that by asserting their business's "special-ness," they've locked themselves into the deadening cycle of having to be present each day to run and control their company. Their belief that their business could never be weaned off its reliance on them, since it is so specialized, complicated, or unique, is one of the most expensive limiting beliefs they could ever accept. It literally costs them millions of dollars of lost growth. What's more, it also costs them their freedom, as they become trapped in the very business they once launched to help them become free.

DAVID'S STORY

They say the first sign of progress is admitting you have a prob-lem—and boy, did I have a problem! I was scared, overwhelmed, and feeling stuck. I didn't understand how to sell or market; I had no skill in how to structure or run a business; and I had no clue how to manage cash flow and build financial controls. I had let my ego-fed pride blind me to my own ignorance and isolate me so I didn't look for the right mentors, advisors, and peer group to guide me.

Going bust helped me to break through my fear-based bravado and understand that I had a lot to learn. And learn I did. I studied. I read. I experimented. I found mentors to teach me, and partners to contribute their best talents. I did what I had done to become an Olympic-level athlete—I got expert-level coaching; I paid attention and focused on learning the key skills that had eluded me the first time around.

The result? Seven years later, I was an "overnight" success—a multimillionaire with two successful companies and a bright entre-preneurial future ahead of me.

But now I had another problem—a serious problem. I was totally burned out and overwhelmed. I was working 70-plus hours a week and was on the road two weeks out of every month. And if that weren't enough, I felt like I was drowning in all the details of running my companies.

Sure, the money was great, but this wasn't what I'd signed up for. I originally started my own company because I wanted to be in control of my destiny. I didn't want to work for anyone else (that is, if anyone else would've had me). I wanted to live my life on my terms, to be the one in charge. But in the end, I wanted one thing more than anything else. In fact, this one thing was the single deep desire that had sparked me to open up shop. It's what drove me to keep going when tough times hit.

I wanted freedom. Freedom from people telling me what to do and how to do it. Freedom to do things my way. Freedom from having my future depend on the whims or decisions of others. And—gulp—time freedom.

Instead of constantly working to feed my business and feeling trapped, I wanted to let my business work for me. The cash flow was great, but I always had to anticipate the pressures of the following month, with its payroll, overhead, necessary sales, and emergencies I knew I'd have to handle.

I wanted out of the pressure cooker, to escape the long hours and ever-present demands. Was it too much to ask for my business to support me instead of me working to support it?

It was at that point I made a decision. I'd build a business that would work without my showing up each day. I focused on it, obsessed over it, took action on it. And little by little, my business started to mature. I found key team members, built strong operational systems, and built a culture that encouraged my team to own much of the day-to-day decision making of running the business.

What happened? Over the next 36 months, we grew our sales from $1 million per year to $6.3 million, and grew our operating profit to $3.2 million. At the same time, by following the same methodology you'll learn in this book, I had reduced my working hours to an average of 35 hours a week and increased my vacation time to three months a year. I was doing the things in the business that I loved out of choice, not obligation, because I'd crafted a role for myself in the company that was both sustainable and enlivening.

At this high point, I received such a good offer for the companies, I decided to accept the offer and sell. I took the money—along with everything I'd learned about building a successful business—and started fresh.

It was then that I realized the most exciting thing of all. The methodology I'd spent years developing to build an owner-independent company worked even better the second and the third time around. I've used it for more than a decade in my various businesses. I've taught it to tens of thousands of entrepreneurs from around the world. And I know it will work for you if you just follow the map in this book.

How Will You Play Today?

We have a belief that the way we do *anything* says a whole lot about the way we do *everything*, that you play like you practice. So how will you play today? How will you approach this book? Will you step up and do the exercises we lay out for you? Will you apply the map we share? Will you take advantage of the extra coaching and tool kit we offer? Or will you say it's just too hard or that you're just too busy?

In life, either you get your excuses or you get your dreams, but you don't get both. Which will it be for you? Decide now. If you're not going to follow the map we lay out for you, then we urge you to give this book to someone else and settle back into your business as it currently is. Why? Because you'll only find the strategies and distinctions you'll read about too intimidating and uncomfortable.

But if you're ready to step up and learn a better way to build your business so you have both the money and the freedom to enjoy it, then turn the page and let's get to work.

FREE BUSINESS OWNER TOOL KIT ($1,375 VALUE)

Because we know how important executing on these ideas is to help you enjoy the growth and freedom you want, we created a special website with a complete tool kit to help you apply what you'll learn in this book and get faster results. This free value add for readers like you includes downloadable PDF versions of the strategy and system creation tools you'll be introduced to in this book, along with dozens of valuable video training sessions and other tools to help you build an owner independent company and get your life back. To get immediate access these tools, just visit **www.MauiMastermind.com/freetoolkit**. (See Appendix A for full details.)

CHAPTER 1

Build
a Business,
Not a Job

In medical school, Bruce learned how to care for patients and help them get the health outcomes they wanted. Of course, nowhere in his four years of medical school, nor in the six years of general surgery training, nor in his two years of plastic surgery training, did he ever get trained on how to best run a medical practice. Imagine that: over a decade of formal advanced education to become a surgeon, and not even *one* course on the business of running a successful practice. So over the two decades after he first opened his surgical practice he just figured it out the best he could.

And by all accounts he was super-successful. He enjoyed a sterling reputation as a talented surgeon, and his practice was highly profitable. But he was tired. Tired of the long days of surgery, fitting in the practice administration on nights and weekends, and missing time with his family. Tired of worrying that if he ever got hurt his practice could very well fail. And tired of feeling trapped in this pressure cooker.

"There was a time, and it wasn't that long ago," Bruce shared, *"when if you had come to me and asked me if I could scale the practice, I would have been concerned that the only way for me to do that would be to work longer hours, performing more surgeries and seeing more patients. I was already working 60 to 70 hours a week and didn't want to work more hours. More than just the hours, I didn't like the fact that I had all of these people, from my family, to my staff, to my patients, who each were counting on me to be there to perform procedures. If I got hurt, or wanted to take some time away from the practice to compete in a*

triathlon, the practice would suffer. The business revenue was so dependent on myself as a single operating surgeon, and there was no end in sight."

To the world, Bruce was a smiling seven-figure surgeon who had it all under control, but inside he craved a way to reduce the practice's reliance on him. He just didn't know how.

What about you? How many hours a week on average do you work for your business? If you're like many of the business owners we've observed, you're working 50 to 70 hours a week or *more*. When you factor in the emails handled from home at odd hours and the calls taken on nights or weekends—not to mention the time spent thinking and worrying about the business when you're away from it—the total hours you work are likely much higher.

According to the Wells Fargo/Gallup Small Business Index, 57 percent of small business owners in the United States work six days a week, and more than 20 percent of them work seven days a week. A recent article in the *Harvard Business Review* reported that the average business owner or professional works an average of 72 hours a week.

Are you still enjoying the business you've built, or has it somehow turned into more of a job? A common myth is that business owners can take time off whenever they want—they control their own schedules, after all. But answer these questions: Could you leave next month for a four-week vacation without harming your business? Would you be checking email and calling the office while you were supposedly on vacation? And what would you find when you returned to the office? Would you find it operating smoothly, with new customers brought in and key deadlines met? Or would you find decisions stalled, projects drifting off course, and fires that needed to be put out? How many weeks of vacation a year have you averaged over the past five years? Were they really vacations or were they times you went away with your family and worked remotely while they enjoyed the beach or cities you traveled to?

Ironically, while one of the drives for most business owners initially was to assert control over their business lives, most later found themselves working longer hours, with less time off, than back when they worked for another company. The sad reality is that the way most business owners have built their companies, they don't have a business; they've built a job for themselves. Sure they get to be the "boss," and sure many of them earn a great living, but that success comes with a hefty price tag—the loss of the deeper sense of control and real freedom they would enjoy *if only they had built a business, not a job.*

Building an Owner-Independent Company

There are three levels for growing an owner-independent business. Here's a quick, high-level overview of this three-level model for scaling your company. Then in later chapters we'll dive progressively deeper into the specific steps and refinements for navigating this map to reach your destination—owning a Level Three owner-independent company.

Level One: The Start-Up—No Control, No Freedom

You've just launched a business.

At this point, not only do you have no freedom because you're working long hours to get things going, but you have no control. You're creating your business plan, gathering your start-up capital, and launching your new venture. Typical Level One business owners are filled with a mixture of doubts and dreams, fears and ambitions. They work long hours scrambling to turn their business idea into a tangible, practical, cash-flowing enterprise.

Level Two: The Owner-Reliant Company—Control, But No Freedom

You're a full-time business owner with a profitable business that works—as long as you are present each day to keep it working.

You make most of the decisions. You generate most of the business. You meet with all the key clients and perform most of the important work of the business. You stay in full control. Sure, you have people to help, but they're there to do just that—help—not to lead or take ownership of central parts of your business.

You have the control, but with that control come long hours and the sense that all the decisions, all the risks, and all the responsibility rest on your shoulders. Every day, you have to keep going because if you stop, it all ends. You have the control, but no real freedom.

Level Three: The Owner-Independent Company—Total Control, Total Freedom

You're the owner of a business that runs without needing your presence and efforts every day.

You've got the team and systems in place so your business's success is independent of you. Working for your business is now a choice, not an obligation or a requirement. At this point you can continue to scale the company, position and sell it, or transition to own it passively.

Decide right now to make building an owner-independent company a stated goal of your business. Start with this end—an owner-independent company—clearly in mind, never wavering from your commitment to build a business that profitably delivers massive value to the market in a highly scalable fashion.

As you'll see as you progress through this book, knowing where you're heading critically changes how you build your business.

Put Your Profits on Autopilot

No doubt you've flown in an airplane. New aviation technology is amazing. As a plane takes off, a highly trained pilot guides it into the air and onto its course, and then turns on the autopilot system. This system maintains the course and manages long stretches of the flight with the pilot keeping an eye on the instrument panel to troubleshoot any problems that might emerge. When the airplane approaches its destination, the pilot again takes over and lands the plane.

Contrast this to a pilot flying an old-fashioned plane without autopilot. Can you imagine the strain of flying cross-country in this type of plane? Sure, it might be exciting the first time, but what if you had to keep flying each day, week after week, month after month, year after year, handling every detail of every flight?

Most business owners build businesses with no autopilot and get stuck for years sitting in the cockpit, straining to maintain the proper control, altitude, and business heading. While many of these business owners make a ton of money, the strain and lifestyle costs are great. We've all seen entrepreneurs who make $1 million or more each year, but they live, breathe, and die by their businesses. We've both *been* those entrepreneurs, unable to get away from our businesses for more than a long weekend here and there. That doesn't feel like success and wealth. Real wealth is when you have money *and* freedom, money *and* quality of life.

The Greatest Challenge Entrepreneurs Face

For the past decade, we've worked with hundreds of thousands of entrepreneurs and business owners, helping them grow their businesses, upgrade their peer groups, and improve their lifestyles. Time after time, we're approached by intelligent, hardworking people who've become owned by the very businesses they once thought *they* owned.

The greatest challenge you'll ever face as an entrepreneur is how to build a business that's independent of you, the business owner.

Take the example of Bonnie Hacker, who founded Emerge, an occupational therapy practice in North Carolina. Bonnie was a gifted occupational therapist who directly helped hundreds of families, personally working to help their children deal with various developmental and behavioral challenges.

"I first started my business because I wanted to help children," Bonnie explains. *"After 15 years in a solo private practice, I wanted to expand what I was doing. I felt drawn to this idea of building a place that could improve the lives of many children and train occupational therapists to provide effective clinic-based therapy. Of course, I didn't know at the start how much of my life it would consume."*

At the time she was first introduced to these business building concepts, Bonnie was working 45 hours a week, and had grown Emerge into a successful $550,000-a-year practice. *"Before I was introduced to these ideas on building an owner-independent company, the biggest headache I dealt with was being responsible for all the staffing issues in the practice. If someone left on maternity leave, it fell to me to cover for them, or if they weren't coming back, to recruit and train their replacement. Then there were the other staff fires that I'd have to put out. It probably consumed 20 hours a month just dealing with this one functional part of the business."*

Does Bonnie's story strike a nerve? Have you ever had to do the "work" of your business during the day, and then fit in the "running the business" responsibilities around your work producing for the company? Not only is this stressful, but it usually hurts the business as you ignore the higher-value work you could do for the business because you're so trapped in the day-to-day role of producing sales, products, or services for your company.

But there is hope. It doesn't have to be this way. Bonnie needed help, and for six years she worked with David's business coaching team to grow and mature her company. Every quarter she worked with David's team to create her 1-page quarterly plan of action for her practice. For six years she dutifully met with her coach every two weeks to gain outside perspective, accountability, and feedback so that she consistently executed on her map to grow her business and reduce its reliance on her. And the outcome? Listen to Bonnie share the amazing difference these ideas—applied and executed in her business—have made over the past six years.

"Here I am six years after diligently applying these business strategies to build an owner-independent practice. I've reduced my working hours to under 10 hours a week, and the practice continues to serve the children we see exceptionally well. At the same time we've grown our revenues by 145 percent to $1,350,000 per year."

It's a Progression, Not an On/Off Switch

As you'll come to learn, building an owner-independent business is a progression, not a light switch you suddenly flip one day. It's not a binary yes/no, but rather a spectrum that you slowly progress through over the course of several years.

The critical shift is from seeing yourself as a *producer* for your business—driving sales and fulfilling client purchases—to seeing yourself as the *builder* of a business that will do all this without you. You're only a temporary producer until you can build the business depth that can replace you.

Let's return to Bruce's story. As a successful surgeon it would be easy for him to see himself as the key driver that makes his business go for- ward—the one irreplaceable ingredient without which the practice would wither and die. Unlike Bonnie, he has been introduced to these ideas and working with David's team for only six months. But even so, during this time, Bruce has made remarkable progress.

He has reduced his working hours in the practice by 10 hours a week. He has increased his operating profit by $270,000 a year and climbing. And he is starting to feel as though there is a pathway for him to scale the practice and get his life back.

"I had 12 years of advanced medical training to become a surgeon, yet I received no training about how to run a successful medical practice. I had to learn by trial and error. Now, with the support and training of my business coach, I'm finally getting that business training. I'm working fewer hours, and actually getting home before the sun sets, which is a real gift. Best of all, I can see the practice becoming stronger and less reliant on me bit by bit each quarter."

Remember, this work is a progression, not an on/off switch. You'll make headway and have temporary reversals, and at times progress will feel slow, almost as if you're pushing uphill. This is normal. But if you persevere, if you stay the course that we'll lay out for you here in this book, you will enjoy greater profits and an improved quality of life.

"In the world of medicine it's a sad fact that the majority of doctors I know end up 20 years into their practice feeling trapped and stuck," Bruce shared. *"Sure they make a great living, but they have to give up so much of their time and life to do it. Maybe you can't make your practice operate completely independently from you, but you can make it much better than it is now. I've seen what a difference working in a structured way on my practice over the past six months has made for me personally. The practice runs more smoothly, it's more profitable, and our staff is happier. Stop making excuses and take that first step."*

STEPHANIE'S STORY

A few years ago, my husband Jack and I took a five-week trip to Italy themed around fine wines and foods. We toured vineyards, took cooking classes, and visited cultural and historic sites throughout Italy.

When we came home, we met with our management team. After they brought us up to speed on the status of key projects and strategic initiatives, they shooed us out the door of the conference room, saying in effect, "We're fine. When is your next trip so we can get back to work?" That day, Jack and I realized we had succeeded in building an owner-independent Level Three business. Our team didn't need us present to operate effectively. In fact, they loved having us gone because that meant they could spread their wings and take more ownership of the process of growing the business.

Now, we don't want to make building an owner-independent Level Three business seem easy, because it's not. While it may be simple when you know how, it will take work, sacrifice, and a deep commitment. But that initial effort directed to building an enterprise that can consistently create and deliver profitable value without you there to run the show is well worth it.

The 7 Major Benefits of Taking Your Business to Level Three

1. **It gives you control over your financial future.** No matter what economic conditions you face, you have the financial strength that allows you to make the choices you want for you and your family. Plus, you have the security that comes from having mastered the skill of how to build a thriving owner-independent Level Three business. Should something happen to one of your

businesses, you have the skills and experience to build another one.

2. **It will massively increase your net worth.** The average owner-independent Level Three business is 10 times more valuable than its Level Two owner-reliant counterpart. Larger revenues mean your company will command a larger multiple if you were to sell it. Plus you'll be a more attractive target for a strategic buyer. Often your business will grow in value *one hundredfold or more* when you take it from Level Two to Level Three.

3. **Your business is much easier to scale.** By its very nature, an owner-independent Level Three business is much easier to scale. It can easily accommodate growth of 50 percent, 100 percent, or more—*per year*. One of our Maui Advisors grew his Level Three business from $10 million to over $100 million in sales in 24 months. Another scaled his company from $100 million to over a *billion dollars* in volume per year in under five years.

4. **You earn your freedom from your business.** It no longer depends on your presence every day to make it work. You have many more options available to you. You get to do the parts of the business you're best at and love most, while letting other people handle the parts you don't enjoy.

5. **An owner-independent Level Three business gives your staff security and growth opportunities.** The business isn't vulnerable to something happening to you, the owner. And as you grow the business and reduce its reliance on your daily presence, you give your staff opportunities to grow and develop as businesspeople as they take on expanded roles in a vibrant, growing enterprise. In fact, all your stakeholders—from staff to suppliers, vendors, investors, and all the people who indirectly rely on your business—will be more secure.

6. **Your business is dramatically more stable.** You're no longer vulnerable if one of your key team members—including yourself—gets hurt or has a life change.

7. **You have a greater impact on your market.** Because it's now scalable, your business is able to create more value for your market as it sells and delivers your products or services to your customers and clients. These products or services improve many people's lives.

Why Do You Want an Owner-Independent Business?

It's been said that with a big enough *why*, you'll always be able to figure out the *how*. We invite you to step back and get clear on *your* why for building a successful business. What would it mean to you if your business were a Level Three business? What would the freedom of owning a Level Three business give you time to pursue? How would you be able to contribute more? What would be the biggest benefit to your family? How would it improve the lives and futures of your employees, vendors, and clients?

Action Time: What are the three strongest drives for you to invest the time, energy, and money to take your business to Level Three?

In other words, looking back over your answers and thinking deeply, what are the three biggest reasons you'll do what it takes to build an owner-independent company? List your top three reasons here.

1. _____

   _____

2. _____

   _____

3. _____

   _____

CHAPTER 2

How the Traditional Model of Building a Business is Flawed

(and What to Do about It)

It had taken a lot of planning and work, but Mark and Diana were finally in Paris—the city of romance, with a rich history and resplendent culture. Diana was so excited to be able to have her husband away from the business and all to herself. But each day of their vacation Diana's heart sank a little bit lower. "All he seemed to do was work remotely *on his laptop from the hotel each day,*" she shared.

Has your significant other or family ever felt that way? Like even when you're with them, you're really not? The core of the problem is likely *how* you've gone about building your business.

The traditional way to build a business is to build an owner-reliant Level Two business. In a Level Two business, you as the business owner gather up the reins of power. All decisions are run past you. You create the plan, you lead the execution of that plan, and you do all the hiring. You meet with all the key clients and perform most of the important work of the business. The staff you have is there to help leverage you, not to lead or take ownership of central parts of your business. If something should happen to you, your business would crumble. And if you somehow manage to escape for a short vacation, you probably sneak your laptop or iPhone® with you on the trip and check email when your spouse and kids aren't looking.

What's the real reason typical owner-reliant Level Two business owners want all the control? They're afraid that if they don't stay in control, things will go wrong. They fear their staff will screw up and the company will lose a customer or face a lawsuit, or even that the company will fail.

So they clutch at the security blanket of control, never seeing that it binds them in their businesses forever.

Remember the scene in *Godfather III* in which Michael Corleone (played by Al Pacino) wants to get out of the family business? He turns to his sister Connie and says, *"Just when I thought I was out, they pull me back in!"* Well, that's exactly how many Level Two business owners feel over time.

While there is nothing wrong with the traditional model, and it works to build a successful Level Two business, it has three serious pitfalls to it.

The 3 Pitfalls of Building Your Business the Level Two Way

Pitfall 1: It caps your income and your success.

If your business revolves around you and your personal production, as you become more successful you'll smack up against the ceiling of how much you personally are able to produce for your business. You can personally do only so much and run only so fast before you just can't do any more.

Take the case of Shirley, owner of two successful Montessori preschools in southern California. Shirley grew these two schools serving 400 children primarily through the traditional model of long hours and hard work. And by the traditional measure of success of a business—profit—she had succeeded. Her schools generated a substantial profit from their roughly $4 million in annual revenues. But Shirley was working herself to death to do it.

"I was working more than 14 hours per day, 7 days a week, and was literally overwhelmed by the business," Shirley reported. *"Much of the work I did, such as greeting the kids and parents and working with a great team of teachers, was satisfying and rewarding. I was, however, the only person able to deal with any escalation that would arise, and with 50 staff members and nearly 400 children enrolled at the two schools, there were many issues to deal with every day. Dealing with all the issues left me exhausted and with little time for working on*

the business, and it was only after the school closed for the day that I could work on the billing, bookkeeping, hiring, HR issues, purchasing, and all the rest."

It was at this point that Shirley was totally maxed out. She literally didn't have any more hours she could work. She was already essentially working 100 hours a week.

Pitfall 2: It puts *everyone* at greater risk.

If you stop working or get injured, your business dies—quickly. This is risky for you, your family, your employees, your customers, and your investors.

We want to ask you an extremely important question, one that very few business owners ever allow themselves to consider because often the answer is too painful to contemplate:

If you were hit by a bus tomorrow (or otherwise incapacitated), what would happen to your business?

We surveyed more than one thousand business owners over the past five years, and our findings revealed that if the average business owner became incapacitated and couldn't work, the business would fail in less than 30 days. Thirty days! Think about what this would mean for the families, employees, and customers. You put in all those years of blood, sweat, and tears to build something that could literally end in less than 30 days.

Let's go back to Shirley. What do you think would have happened to her two schools if Shirley had been "hit by a bus"? The schools would have failed and been closed or sold in a fire sale. Her staff would have lost their jobs. And all those children would have lost their schools, forcing their parents to scramble to find childcare for their kids. Everyone would have lost out.

Pitfall 3: It eventually corners you in the Self-Employment Trap— the more success you have, the more trapped you become inside your business.

You're so busy doing the "job" of your business that you can't step back and grow and develop your business as a *business*. What's more, because of the way you've built an owner-reliant company, the more success you have growing the business based on your personal production and personal participation, the more you become trapped inside the business. It quite literally *can't* function without you.

Remember, being caught in the Self-Employment Trap is not a function of the size of your business; it's a direct result of the model with which you choose to build your company. Whether you're running a small three-person professional practice, a medium-sized 50-person organization like Shirley's, or a large 312-person manufacturing company, if you build the company by keeping all the key decisions and direct control in your hands you'll likely end up stuck in the Self-Employment Trap. It's only by working to build your company independent of you (and independent of any key staff member) that you will be able to escape and get your life back.

Escaping the Self-Employment Trap

In the traditional approach to building your business, you try to grow by personally working harder and producing more. You make the decisions. You stay in control. Your team runs everything important past you first. But the problem is that it's like stepping on a treadmill and simply running faster. And as you go faster, you increase the speed of the treadmill. You take on more overhead, hire more employees, and make more client commitments, all of which merely increase the pressure you feel to personally produce more. And what happens if you ever stop running now that your base speed on the treadmill is so high? You come crashing off the end of the treadmill and your business dies.

So what's the way out of the Self-Employment Trap? You can't just work harder; you've got to run your business *smarter*. This means that rather than just working harder and doing more, you've got to do *less* and get your *business* to produce more. Remember, the more you do, the more you have to keep doing. The more you get your business to do, the less you have to do personally, freeing up your time to grow and build your business.

"If you had asked me before I started the business coaching pro- gram if I could have ever let go of the feeling that I needed to person- ally perform or control every aspect of my business," Shirley shared, *"I would have told you no. What I realize now is that, while I am a great contributor to the business, if I build it all around me, I am its greatest limitation. To grow and serve more children and families, I need to be willing to let my team shine. Of course we need the structured systems and a sound culture to guide the team, but the business needs to be able to be successful without me. Letting go hasn't been easy for me, but it has been so worthwhile. Because of the changes I have made to my beliefs and to the systems and controls we have put in place, I have more time for my family and have greatly reduced the stress in my life."*

Building an owner-independent Level Three business is a lot like raising kids. Immediately after birth and for the first few years, you put in a tremendous amount of care and feeding, not to mention changing a few diapers! This requires lots of your time. Of course it does. Just as in the early years of your business, you're naturally the main engine driving your business forward. You'll wear all the hats at various times, and you'll have few formal structures and systems within your organization upon which you can truly rely. But as it matures—like when your kids start school—you create some breathing space.

As you enter Level Two, you'll face a crucial decision point at which you can settle for owning a Level Two "job," or instead choose to raise your business to be a strong owner-independent Level Three business that benefits from your involvement but is ultimately independent of it. Just like your goal as a parent is raising kids who can eventually stand on their own—independent and self-supporting—so your goal is to create an organization with the systems, team, controls, and culture that allow it to stand on its own.

The 8 Building Blocks of All Owner-Independent Businesses

Every owner-independent Level Three business is built with eight essential building blocks:

1. Systems
2. Team
3. Controls
4. Scalable solutions
5. Culture
6. Strategic structure
7. Coherence
8. Accountability

Let's look at each of these eight building blocks in turn.

#1: Systems—The Backbone of Your Owner-Independent Business

Systems are reliable processes and procedures that empower your business to consistently produce an excellent result for your clients or customers. They're documented best practices that increase your company's efficiency and reduce costly mistakes. Systems include documents and processes such as the checklists your fulfillment department follows to ensure that all orders are shipped correctly, the orientation process for all new clients when you begin working together, the standardized contracts you use with all your new vendors, and even the checklists you use before you bring any new hire on board. Your business systems include any company know-how captured in a tangible format versus locked in the brain of an individual team member that enables the business to get consistently great results.

Remember Bonnie, whose story we shared in the last chapter? When Bonnie first began working with David's business coaching company, it became painfully obvious after the first few months that the office manager running the administrative and billing side of her business wasn't the right fit for the practice. And while it's never easy to let a team member go, Bonnie knew her company needed someone else in that key role.

It took her almost two months to gather her courage and break the news to this staff member. During that time, Bonnie realized that most of the knowledge for how to run the back office in the practice wasn't formally captured in any systems or documentation, but existed in her own head as well as the head of this office manager. We coached Bonnie on how best to let her office manager go and use onboarding and orienting her new hire as an opportunity to systematize this critical role's core functions.

Bonnie wrote a clear job description for the position. She wrote out the step-by-step procedures for onboarding a new client, including collating all new client documentation with filled-out samples so any team member could walk a new client through the process. She redesigned her billing procedures to make sure clients were charged the right amounts at the right times. She documented the therapist scheduling processes and the other key back-office functions. Then when she hired Lauren into this role, Bonnie took the time to train Lauren in these systems, empowering her to refine and improve these initial systems that Bonnie had created.

In the end, Bonnie reduced her business's reliance on any one person in the office manager's role, and she improved the practice's administrative and billing performance by creating clear systems and training Lauren on these systems. In fact, she increased the practice's cash flow by more than $50,000 per year by correcting all the prior billing mistakes she found when closely reviewing the former office manager's performance.

How much of your business know-how is locked away in the brains of others? What if you lose one or more of these team members? What can you do in the next 90 days to reduce your business's vulnerability if any of them were to leave, including you?

The Discipline of Creating Systems

Building systems is a team effort and a discipline. You'll need to train your team to create, organize, use, fine-tune, and, if need be, eliminate your business systems. Many of your new team members will have little or no training in the importance, creation, and refinement of systems. In fact, some will see systems as a hassle or an impediment. It's your job to help them recognize how useful systems can be to get their jobs done— and how critical they are to the long-term success of the business. One of your key responsibilities is to establish the discipline and culture of creating and using systems in your organization.

You won't set this up all at once; rather, it's a cumulative process that takes place over time. We'll come back to this process again in more detail throughout this book. For now, we simply want to introduce you to the need for systems and to prime you to look at your business through a systems-reliant filter. It's our intention to spark in you the desire to no longer settle for one-off efforts of yourself or key employees, but to instead establish system-driven solutions.

The 2 Layers to Every Successful Business System

Every successful business system has two layers: the process layer and the format layer.

The *process layer* consists of the step-by-step process or procedure you've created. Does your system accurately capture the steps of the process so that when you follow it you consistently get the desired result? It does you no good to formalize poor processes. You want your systems to capture your best practices and winning moves, making it easier for your company to replicate and scale those successes.

The *format layer* deals with how you package and present your system to your team. Is your system easy to use? Is it transparent so team members intuitively understand how to use it? Can it be automated so much of the work happens via technology instead of manual work? For example, this could be automated reporting built into your database to track sales or monitor client orders. It could also be enterprise software that your team uses to run the entire flow of your business, featuring key systems built directly into the software. Or it could be simple, low-tech tools like a script for your scheduling assistant to use when he or she leaves a message for people, or a standardized form that your receptionist gives each new client to fill out upon arriving for an appointment.

Done right, systems make life easier for your team and success more predictable for your business.

A Simple Test to Know If You Got Your System's Format Correct

Having a solid process isn't enough. You have to package that process in ways that your team will actually use.

How do you know if your system has a good, usable format?

Ask one simple, unambiguous, incontrovertible question: *Is your team using it?* The real test is whether your team embraces it, ignores it, or, even worse, creates a shortcut system for the task.

Your team members want to do a good job. If your business systems are simple, intuitive, and effective, they will use them. If they're confusing, complicated, bloated, or cumbersome, they'll ignore these systems and even create their own "cheat sheet" hybrid versions instead. But these homespun, individual hybrids normally aren't scalable. In fact, they usually work only for that one team member and only as long as the volume of your business stays relatively level. Plus, even if this private shortcut works, rarely is it ever captured in a way that the rest of your business can use it. And when that team member goes, so does that know-how.

To get the format layer right, watch the way your team members use, or don't use, your systems. Don't argue, don't preach, don't cajole—simply observe. Take their behavior as critical feedback to refine and improve your systems. Remember, those systems are meant to leverage, empower, and simplify the lives of your employees, so don't fall in love with any specific system. Rather, fall in love with the result it's intended to generate.

25 EFFECTIVE FORMATS TO PACKAGE YOUR SYSTEMS

Here is a quick list of 25 potential formats for you to package your systems to make them easier and more effective for team members to use.

1. Checklists
2. Scripts
3. Worksheets
4. Step-by-step instructions
5. Software that automates a process
6. Databases of key information
7. Pricing lists
8. Templates and samples
9. FAQs
10. Written warnings for an area, providing how to deal with predictable problems
11. Spreadsheets with built-in formulas
12. Camera-ready art files
13. Filing system (paper or electronic)
14. Preapproved vendors lists
15. Standardized equipment and parts
16. Online communication tools for effectively sharing information (discussion forums, wikis, whiteboards, social networks, etc.)
17. Delivery timetables
18. Job descriptions
19. Instructional videos
20. Project management software with reusable project pathways
21. Reporting templates
22. Organizational charts
23. Preapproved forms and contracts
24. A timeline or Master Calendar
25. Complete enterprise management software

As business owners ourselves, we understand that implementing systems is a key ingredient to help us scale. What isn't always obvious is how precisely to do this. What formats work best for what types of systems?

Here are three types of situations you may need a system to help handle, along with a list of the potential best formats for your systems to handle those situations.

Situation One: A system to coordinate activities between multiple people

(For example, to produce a product or deliver a service, get an outside vendor to do a complicated process or deliver a key service to your company, or make a joint venture event flow smoothly.)

- **A defined timeline:** This lets all players visually see the sequencing of steps and stages in a way that they can integrate into their personal calendars.

- **A flowchart of the process steps:** Not only does this let you better organize and optimize the process, but it makes key dependencies clear and gives all players in the system a better understanding of how their work fits into the bigger picture.

- **A project "task list":** Built like a checklist, this tool helps you clarify explicitly who needs to do what, by when.

- **An event "screenplay":** When watching a play, the audience isn't aware that the stage manager has in front of him or her a detailed scene-by-scene three-ring binder that lists out exactly which props are being used and where they are placed, who are in which scenes (and where they enter onto the stage, and the lighting and sound cues that will happen and when). Done as a progressive timeline, this is like a timeline on steroids. For example, David's company, Maui Mastermind, produces multiple high-end business owner training workshops each year. Their event "screenplay" lays out exactly what props go where, which hand- outs need to be given to participants and when, and what audiovisual needs are for each segment. This allows the company to consistently produce five-star business training events, and to have protection should a key staff member need to miss an event due to personal reasons.

Situation Two: A system to guarantee all the steps in a complicated process are followed

(For example, to produce a valuable service, ship a complicated order accurately, or implement a key marketing strategy.)

- **A comprehensive checklist:** As long as all the boxes are checked, your company can be confident that all the steps were followed.

- **A procedural recipe:** This is simply a complete detailed list of all the steps in the process, in order. This is very useful to capture key company knowledge, when training a new team member, or when working to optimize a process. But be aware that once a team member is fluent with a process, he or she will likely just ignore this long, intimidating written-out process.

- **A "cheat sheet" version checklist:** For people who do a process over and over, this shorthand version will give them the mental anchor to make sure all the key steps are taken, in order, but not be so overloaded with nonessential information that your staff might be tempted to skip over it. For example, think of the checklists that pilots use for various situations. They are condensed down and rely on the pilot being trained in the background expertise to wield each of these checklists for a specific outcome. Airlines know that if they were to give their pilots a 27-page version of the checklist most wouldn't use it.

- **Technology automation:** Remember that anything that can be automated is one of your best ways to make sure all the needed steps in a complicated process are in fact being followed. If it can be reduced to software, and that software can be checked and double-checked, then you now have an exceptionally scalable way to handle that portion of your system.

- **Templates:** When you template a complicated process (or more likely, when you template a portion of that complicated process), you build much of the expertise into that template. It's a great form of embedded control to protect your company as you scale.

Situation Three: A system to capture key company know-how that has been painfully gained through expensive trial and error
(For example, pricing information and agreements for key vendors, client project histories, or sales product knowledge and scripting.)

- **A database of key information:** This could be a spreadsheet with vendor pricing, a customer relationship management (CRM) file with all key customer emails and customer notes, or even a project management folder or workspace tool housing all key contracts, task checklists, and work papers.

- **A template of key work output:** As we shared earlier, templates are a great way to capture expert knowledge. These could include a "request for proposal" template, a standardized "bid" template, or a "new client record in CRM" template.

- **Standardized system tools:** These could include formatted spreadsheets with built-in (and proofed) formulas, diagnostic decision trees to help a team member visually approach a situation, or even a simple worksheet that prompts your team to record all the key information in an organized way. This could also include standardized sales scripting or proven marketing collateral.

- **FAQs:** These are a great way to list out in a searchable format the most common questions and their respective answers about key areas of your business. You could have FAQs that explain how to do your monthly client invoicing, describe product features and benefits, or even explain how to follow up with the project team.

- **Formal project debriefing sessions:** If you do a lot of brainwork to produce your product or service offering, then consider regular debriefing sessions during which you pull key team members into a conference room and run through a structured series of questions with the aim of capturing new insights, best practices, improvements, expensive failures to learn from, and the like from your team that performed that work. Then make sure you store and share that information in standardized ways. For example, consider sending out a two-page "project write-up" to your entire team after a key project closes with the top insights (perhaps with links to more detailed information that came out of your debriefing).

We'll go deeper into systematizing your business in Chapter 4, including sharing with you a powerful tool called your "Ultimate Business System" (UBS) that will give you a concrete starting point to engage your whole company in building, using, and refining your systems.

#2: Team—The Leverage Point to Enroll the Unique Talents of Other People

Every business needs talented people to help make it successful. Our insistence that your business's success be independent of any one person does *not* mean your team is unimportant. On the contrary, the only way to build an owner-independent Level Three business is to have *great* team members who consistently perform for your company. It's critical, however, to ensure that your company doesn't rely on the presence of any one individual. Instead, make key team members responsible for creating the systems to do their individual jobs and groom their successors and backups.

Let's return to Mark and Diana for a moment. One of the key things that allowed Mark to grow his company by over 100 percent to sales of $1.6 million per year, while at the same time reducing his working hours in half to 35 hours a week, was learning to give more ownership and responsibility of key functions to his team. This wasn't an easy step for Mark to take. He, like other business owners, had his share of painful experiences of delegating responsibilities to his staff members only to later learn that deliverables fell through the cracks and mistakes were made. But here's the thing—when you combine a strong team member with the structure of solid systems, you grow your company's capability to get things done independent of you.

When two years ago Mark surprised his wife Diana with a second trip to Paris, Diana confesses that she didn't even want to go. Memories of that first trip and the disappointment she felt as Mark spent all his time in the hotel working lingered. But she decided to give Mark a second chance and they went. The first day in Paris Mark started to follow his old pattern of checking his email from his laptop in the hotel. Diana watched this and thought to herself, *"Here we go again."*

But this time Mark's *business* was different. When he started to answer emails and respond to client questions, Mark got a polite but firm email from his new office manager telling him to enjoy his vacation, and that the team had him covered. After Mark's second attempt at working remotely, his office manager playfully upped the ante by telling Mark that if he didn't stop working on his vacation she would be forced to *"suspend his email account."* She reassured him that if an emergency came up they would reach out to him, but that his team, the team he had worked so diligently over the prior two years to build, could handle the routine operation of the business during his two-week vacation. Talking with Diana upon their return she shared, *"We had an amazing time. After our office manager called Mark out on his behavior he and I had an incredible time."*

Take an honest look at your company. Have you built and developed the team that could, given the proper systems, handle the day-to-day operation of your company? Have you helped them build the confidence to "own" parts of the business? Do they feel empowered to make appropriate decisions and take necessary actions without running everything past you first? If not, what are you going to do about it?

#3: Controls—Intelligent Checks and Balances That Put Your Business in Control (Not You)

Cheryl ran a $1.5 million per year glass company. She worked hard, typically 70 hours a week, and she was scared to death to empower her team to own functions and responsibilities within the business.

"David," she said, *"I've tried that before. I delegated to my team and asked them to run their respective areas of the business, and after six months my business was a mess. Sure we had grown, but our margins had shrunk, customers weren't happy, and I hated the stress of waiting to see what would go wrong next."*

In Cheryl's world, the reason her experiment with empowerment didn't work was that she gave up control and her team just wasn't capable enough to do things as well as she could.

So her solution was to just grab back the reins and take charge of the company in a firm manner.

And it worked, to a degree. She improved margins and grew profits. But then she hit a plateau where she was stuck—for several years. What was worse, she was working harder than ever, stretched thin and unable to even think about growing any more for fear of things coming crashing down again.

What had she missed? Was it really a choice between "stay in tight control of everything but accept long hours, heavy stress, and a ceiling on your growth" or "delegate responsibility but know that something bad will happen"?

Cheryl didn't understand that the problem wasn't that she let go of control, but rather that the real problems her company suffered were a direct result of *how* she let go of control. She merely handed control over to team members, with no way for the business to make sure that the staff members she delegated authority to were doing a great job. And when things went wrong, she reverted back to that traditional owner-reliant Level Two mode of running her business.

Think of it this way. *You* don't need to be in control; you need your *business* to be in control. What's the difference? When you are in control, you need to be present daily to exercise that control. When your business is in control, it operates with a solid foundation of systems, processes, and procedures to address the *business's* needs, not just your fears and limitations as the owner.

Controls are the intelligent processes, procedures, and safeguards that protect your company from uninformed or inappropriate decisions or actions by any team member. When you build a business versus a job, you want your team to have the authority to get tasks done without running everything past you. You need them to exercise their judgment and use their discretion. But you also need to empower them with the feedback, ground rules, and double checks they need to do their best work. This is where business controls come into play.

Building strong internal controls is not about you, the business owner, being in control, but rather enhancing and giving control to your business. The best controls make the default behavior the right behavior. And they empower your team to get better results with less effort by giving them immediate feedback and a more defined playing field.

Controls are not about you being a traffic cop hiding in the bushes to leap out and give an unwary team member a speeding ticket; rather, you want your controls to be more like a speedometer or cruise control system that helps individual team members autonomously do better work. Your controls, which are really just a specialized subset of your business systems, help your team members do better work.

Further, good controls also empower your managers and leaders with immediately clear and actionable information on how to coach and redirect your team, by letting them know what's going on in an area at any given moment.

35 Business Controls Most Businesses Need

Let's talk specifics. Here are 35 examples of business controls in five categories that most businesses will eventually need to get to Level Three.

As you read this list, understand that it isn't comprehensive—but it provides a sense of what we mean by business controls. Also, don't stress out thinking you need to build in all these controls *this quarter.* Accept that building in controls is a work in progress to be implemented over time.

Financial Controls

When it comes to the topic of controls, no subject is more emotionally charged than financial controls. Business owners fear possible financial abuses and mistakes if they don't personally control the money in the business.

Take a look at 10 sound financial controls that are both scalable and powerful in protecting your enterprise from financial abuses. Again, the list is not comprehensive, but it provides one view of what controls can look like.

1. **Have more than one person involved in any one cycle of money.** This is an essential "check and balance." Having two or more people sign off on all money flows and money cycles reduces temptation and makes fraud or theft less likely. Here are a few examples:

   a. Person A logs in checks and cash; person B verifies the math and makes the deposit.

   b. Person A deposits the money; person B reconciles the bank statements.

   c. Person A writes out the checks; person B reviews and signs them.

2. **Thoroughly check employees and independent contractors *before* you hire them.** Do a criminal background check on each one and, if they handle money in any form, a credit check, too. Verify employment history and talk with past references, confirming that these references are real.

3. **Reduce liquid cash, which is always a temptation.** Get cash out of the system ASAP and with great care and attention. Here are a few examples of what you can do:

   a. Replace petty cash with a reimbursement system.

   b. If an employee collects cash from a customer, have that cash immediately deposited the same day with two people involved in that cycle of money flow.

   c. Get machines that take credit cards versus only coins and bills.

4. **Have appropriate balances accessible in operating accounts, and keep other monies in one or more segregated accounts with tighter financial controls.** This lowers your exposure yet allows you to give access to small accounts with appropriate controls to staffers who need operating money.

5. **For purchasing decisions, formally set levels of spending authority for your team.** For example, if the expense is less than $1,000, no approval is needed, but supporting documentation and receipts must be filed with the area manager. If the expense is more than $1,000 but less than $5,000, the area manager must approve the expense in advance. If the expense is more than $5,000...You get the idea.

6. **Establish formal refund and return policies that spell out who is and is not authorized to make refunds.** Spell out which kinds of refunds each has the authority to do.

7. **Determine safeguards for customer credit cards and other financial information.** For example, lock all file cabinets, shred trash daily, and use password protection on computer databases.

8. **Create a formalized expensing system.** This would include a list of expenses that are and are *not* reimbursable, as well as a standardized expense report that team members must use. Include a space on that form for the person to sign, declaring that the expenses submitted are true and accurate. Require that receipts be attached for all expensed items.

9. **Get to know your business and the key numbers so you can quickly see what's normal and what's not.** Encourage your management team to understand the same. Make it a core value of your business to immediately red flag anything that seems strange. Follow up on all red flags immediately. Here are some examples:

   • *Key ratios:* Check your cost of goods sold ratio, net income percentages, gross margins, and other relevant financial ratios for your business on a regular basis. These should stay consistent. If they vary or look abnormal, find out why.

   • *Key expenses:* If you don't recognize a vendor, if you suspect an expense is out of line, or if you see income anomalies, investigate immediately.

- *Key rough checks:* Look at the indirect ways of ballparking your financial numbers to corroborate that things are in line with what's normal. For example, compare inventory turns to sales figures, compare staff hours to sales volume, and so on.

10. **Obtain the right kind of insurance and bonding coverage if appropriate.** You can learn more about financial controls, including accessing a complimentary 47-minute training video called, *"43 Must Have Financial Controls to Protect Your Company from Fraud, Embezzlement, and Simply Dumb Mistakes"* as part of the free Business Owner Tool Kit. Go to **www.MauiMastermind.com/freetoolkit**. (See Appendix A for details.)

Operational Controls

11. **Manage costs and expenditures** with approved operating budgets.

12. **Manage client fulfillment** with production schedules and checklists of deliverables.

13. **Monitor client satisfaction** with follow-up surveys and informal interviews.

Marketing Controls

14. **Establish and follow a Master Marketing Calendar** that lays out key deadlines and review dates to make sure your marketing campaigns stay on track.

15. **Create visual scorecards for key marketing metrics** (e.g., cost per lead, cost per sale, net leads per lead source, etc.).

16. **Establish a formal approval process** for your quarterly marketing plan, creative artwork, and other key marketing output early in the process before you spend too much time or money on them.

17. **Have a checklist your team follows** when promoting an event or launching a marketing campaign.

Sales Controls

18. **List negotiating parameters your sales team can work within out in the field.** Examples might be preapproved concessions your sales team can use to close a sale, discounts or credits your frontline staff

are authorized to give when dealing with a purchasing customer in your store, and so on.

19. **Establish an approval process for sales exceptions.** For example, if a concession is worth less than $X, the sales manager must verbally approve it; if a concession exceeds that amount, the sales manager must physically sign off on it.

20. **Require standardized sales paperwork and contracts.**

21. **Provide the sales team with formalized sales scripting.**

22. **Require employment contracts that protect the proprietary nature of your client list.** Possibly parcel out access to that database among the salespeople so that they never have access to more of that list than they actually need.

23. **Require salespeople to use only company-controlled contact phone numbers, email addresses, social media accounts, and so on with clients.** They should never be expected or allowed to give out personal contact information; all contact should flow through company-controlled contact mechanisms.

24. **Provide a direct line for client feedback** that doesn't allow salespeople to filter out negative messages.

25. **Record clear and accurate sales metrics.** These would include daily dials made, number of customer visits per week, closing ratios, retention rates, return rates, net referral score, and so on.

Metrics and Scorecards

A scorecard, sometimes called a "dashboard," is a simple visual way to measure how a key area of your business if performing. It's like looking up at the scoreboard of an athletic event and seeing the time remaining, the scores of both teams, and who has possession of the ball.

Quantitative data gives your entire team a simple, clear, objective way to measure the performance of an area of your business. If the numbers show you're off course, your scorecard can flash a yellow or red alert to your team so they can remediate the situation.

Here are examples of metrics your business may want to measure on its scorecards.

26. **Gross margins:** (*Total Sales* minus *Cost of Sales*) divided by *Total Sales.*

27. **Number of new leads into business per day, week, or month.**

28. Cost per lead by lead source: *Total Number of Leads by Lead Source* divided by *Total Cost of Generating Those Leads by Lead Source.*

29. Average unit of sale: *Total Gross Sales* divided by *Total Number of Customer Orders.*

30. Average time to process new orders.

31. Return rate by product category.

32. Defects per 1,000 parts.

33. On-time delivery rate.

34. Average number of days before you turn your inventory.

35. Ratio of actual expenses to budgeted expenses.

You may be thinking that business controls sound like formalized business systems, and you're right. Every key control is, in reality, a defined, formalized business system so that checks and balances aren't left to chance but are built into the structure of the business. This protects your company and allows you to have peace of mind, even when you let go of direct control over a process, action, or decision.

In fact, this was one of the biggest reasons Cheryl got into such trouble when she simply handed authority over to her team. She didn't realize that letting go of control wasn't an on/off switch—stay in control completely/let go completely; rather, it was a dimmer with which she needed to progressively ease ownership of functions to her staff, with each key function having a structure of system and controls to it.

She had no feedback process to let her business, including the individual performing the work, her managers supervising the work, and herself as the C-suite leader supervising her managers, know if things were being done the right way, at the right time, getting the right result.

If she'd had better controls and structured systems, and eased the delegation of authority and control over to her team in a more intentional and strategic way, she would have avoided most of the chaos and expensive mistakes that her company suffered when she ceded control. Instead she abdicated responsibility to her team, didn't empower them with the right systems framework, and couldn't see how things were progressing until it was too late. When things came crashing down, rather than taking a good, hard look at *how* she had tried to let go of control, she panicked and grabbed control back, shrinking her company by

50 percent to a size she felt she could personally oversee and maintain direct control of. This knee-jerk reaction trapped her inside the business working long hours with lots of stress and pressure to personally produce more.

Contrast Cheryl's story with the experience of Steve, one of David's business coaching clients. Steve was the co-owner of a successful online retailer and wholesaler of electronics. At the time Steve first enrolled in the business coaching program, his company had annual sales of $5 million. But the company was stuck because he kept spending too much time managing the day-to-day details of the operational area of the business. He struggled with the idea that he could step away from that level of involvement without too many mistakes being made and his business suffering. He got it *intellectually* that he needed to extricate himself by building systems and empowering his team, but just couldn't swallow it *emotionally*.

His business sold millions of dollars' worth of electronic parts every year, and each time that he got involved in the fulfillment end of boxing, testing, or moving parts, or in the direct supervision of these activities, it cost his business thousands of dollars in lost revenue. Why? Because it took Steve away from doing those things in the business wherein he could contribute the most value to progress the company toward its top goals. For Steve's company, that meant having him focus on creating the sales systems that would sell more electronic parts, and the purchasing system that would get better pricing from suppliers. These two functions were a magnitude more valuable to his company than him stalking the warehouse floor, spot-checking shipments. But he let his drive for control crowd out this better choice.

After a few months of coaching, along with the positive peer pressure from other business owners in the program who encouraged Steve to move past his compulsion to maintain control, he made the stretch commitment to *"not pick up any piece of equipment in the warehouse"* and to get himself out of *all* day-to-day operations by year-end. This was a huge leap of faith on Steve's part, and one that scared him to death.

At first he went through withdrawal symptoms. He stressed over what was being missed. But as he stepped back and looked at the reporting that his internal systems and controls generated, he began to calm down. He realized not only that things *weren't* falling apart, but that his team was more productive as they gained more control themselves.

It took him 10 months to get himself 95 percent out of the operations area of the business. This saved him 25 hours a week, which he was then able to reinvest in growing his sales force and improving the marketing systems. Over the following 48 months he increased sales to over $20 million per year. This wouldn't have been possible if he hadn't turned over the details of the company's operations to his team, using the systems and controls they jointly developed and refined.

#4: Scalable Solutions—Removing Barriers and Unnecessary Constraints

Have you ever watched the television show *This Old House*? Imagine you're on it, working on a 75-year-old house with its original electrical wiring and plumbing. What would happen if you plugged in a full complement of modern electrical appliances? You'd blow your fuses, not to mention create the potential for an electrical fire to break out. And what would happen to your plumbing if you went from a well-water system to tapping into the higher pressure of city water? (Can you say rain gear?)

Likewise, too much growth that makes increasing demands on old, outdated systems is what causes most growing businesses to fail. The systems that worked for a $500,000-a-year business are no longer sufficient to cope with a $5 million business, and not even close to being adequate for a $50 million business. At first, the additional sales will cause a few "leaks," but before long, your business will have burst pipes and water everywhere. That's where the building block of scalable solutions comes into play.

Morgan was a young man in his late 20s when he started his mortgage brokerage company, Morgan Financial. He built a successful owner-reliant company for himself with one office in Portland, Oregon. After a few years, Morgan took the scary step of opening a second office. It turned out to be profitable, and for a time he settled back enjoying the results of his two offices. If that were the end of Morgan's ambitions, the story would have ended like it does for most small-business owners— with Morgan settling into his 30- to 40-year role of running his two-office mortgage business as a self-employed business owner, working 50, 60, or 70 hours a week, struggling to take any substantial time away from the business.

And for years, that's the business he was satisfied with—two offices helping home buyers get mortgages. That was until he met a key mentor named Doug. About 10 years older than Morgan, Doug had built up several successful companies. Doug saw something in Morgan and decided to work with him to scale his company. Doug provided the capital, confidence, and counsel that Morgan needed to scale his business.

Over the next eight years, Morgan went from two offices with a handful of staff to 212 offices and 1,000 team members in 23 states doing over $1 billion of loans annually. Morgan made the first leap from one to two offices by himself in four years. With the help of his mentor, he went from two to 212 offices—a *one hundredfold* increase—over the next eight years.

DAVID'S STORY

Many business owners say that because they're selling expertise that lives in their heads, they can't scale their businesses. This is especially true of the professional practices we coach. These doctors, lawyers, and highly paid consultants say, *"David, there's no way we can scale. We can see how what you teach would apply to* other *businesses,* other *industries,* other *models, but not to ours."*

Then I point them to examples of other clients of ours in their same industry who've substantially grown their companies and increased their personal freedom at the same time. I ask them to look for examples of other professional practices they know who've made the leap to an owner-independent company. It's at this point that they start to open their minds.

Then I give them the direct example of my business coaching company, Maui Mastermind, which when you look deeply has had to face and solve the exact same challenge they face—how to replicate and scale in a profitable and consistently excellent way the expert-reliant skill of coaching a company to successfully scale.

The secret is that if you are willing to challenge the assumption that only you, the world-class expert that you are—whether this be in medicine, or in IT infrastructure, or in accounting, or in law—can help your clients get whatever results or outcome they came to you for, then you can find scalable ways to better serve your clients.

Two decades ago when I first began coaching business owners I was the coach. And I helped my clients get great results, customizing my approach to that individual's business situation and needs.

Over the past 20 years we've captured our methodology in a concrete, comprehensive coaching system that works for a broad range of businesses. Over time we've taken the feedback from working with thousands of coaching clients to refine our core process. At this point we're probably on coaching system 210.0. Not only have we had a large number of clients who've helped us sharpen our methodology, but we've had dozens of capable, experienced business coaches who've helped us hone our system along the way. This large body of clients and coaching talent, combined with a commitment to build a scalable model that can serve thousands of businesses, has helped us get to the coaching program we have today.

While we're not done improving yet, nor will we ever be, the program as it exists today is by every measure we track *more* effective and valuable to our clients. Our average client today enjoys an annual growth rate of 64.2 percent per year, double the annual growth rate we helped clients achieve several years ago, and *9 times greater* than the average growth rate of the typical privately owned company in the United States. And at the same time our average client increases his or her company's "Owner Independence Index" by 97.4 percent per year, 20 percent better than our success rate years ago.

And while I do personally still coach a small stable of clients, most of whom have been with me for *years*, the vast majority of our coaching clients work with our coaching staff to get these results. How is this possible?

Sure, we found talented coaches; no doubt about that. **But the real secret was to build the "secret sauce" into the system itself.** How many coaching sessions each month should we do? How long is the optimal session? What are the best coaching formats and interventions to make these coaching sessions produce maximum impact? What tools do we need to empower our clients to build a business, not a job? What in- person, live training schedule leads to the best outcome? How do we best involve a client's staff so that he or she has us coaching the team to implement these methodologies and strategies to improve the business? All of this is baked into the coaching system itself. Again, as I just shared, this is never going to be a finished product, because we can constantly find ways to refine, improve, redesign, and enhance the program.

This is something too many business owners who have a business wherein they are selling their expertise don't realize—the very process of systematizing your expert way of doing something helps you to improve the value you deliver to your client or patient, both by refining your methodology *and* by improving the consistency and quality of how you implement, apply, and transfer that value to your clients.

This is why when you're building your internal structures—your systems and controls—you look for ways to choose scalable options. This also includes the strategic choices you make as to your business model, market served, staffing decisions, product or service lines to focus on, and more. By doing this, you remove the past constraints to growth and give yourself a much bigger potential future to grow into.

As you can imagine, the systems and structure that helped Morgan run his two-location company were not the systems he needed and eventually had to develop to run his 212-location company.

Scaling your business requires building it in such a way that your model and systems can be rolled out and replicated on a much bigger playing field. When you're solving a business challenge, you must look for solutions that can be scaled. For example, imagine you were building a web platform to process orders from your field sales force. When evaluating which platform to purchase, a Level Three thinker would choose one that could handle the high transaction volume you eventually want to have, provided the cost for this greater capacity isn't too high. If the cost doesn't make financial sense, consider a smart alternative. Choose a plat-form that can be easily upgraded later as your sales volume increases and you have the excess cash flow to warrant the upgrade. You'd say "no" to any platform that couldn't handle your expected sales volume or be easily upgraded and expanded later.

#5: Culture—The Hidden Hand That Shapes Your Team's Behavior

Obviously sound systems and intelligent internal controls are two major ingredients to build a company that is owner independent. **But what happens when a novel situation comes up for which you don't have a system to detail out how you want your team to respond?** This is where your company's culture can save the day.

Your company's culture is the sum total of the absorbed values and unstated "way we do things around here." If it is built wisely, it will help your team handle novel situations that you have no system to outline. One way to think about culture is that it is the invisible hand that shapes your team's behaviors when no one is looking.

Here are six tips to help you and your leadership team establish and reinforce your company culture.

1. **Concretely write out a vision of what you want your company's culture to be.**
   Before you can establish, let alone reinforce, your company's culture, you need to get clear on what you want your culture to be.

   Over the next 30 days, set aside a few 45- to 60-minute blocks of time to just journal on paper what you want your company's culture to look like. What values would people internalize? How would these internalized values show up in their behavior? What would an outside observer notice about the feel of your company if the observer spent the day in your offices?

   Gut Check: How does your company currently line up on your vision of what you want your culture to be? Imagine you were an outsider looking in. Where would you notice things aligning or not aligning between the observed culture and your desired culture?

   Take this feedback and use it to refine your written vision of your company culture. Talk with your team about this vision. Get their thoughts and input. This is a process that unfolds over several months, not just in a "sit down one time" event.

2. **Celebrate victories and behavior in alignment with your core values and brand immediately.**
   Highlight the great behavior; celebrate the story of the success. The closer you make the celebration to the behavior, the more you reinforce the desired value. Over time it is these small steps that accumulate into your culture.

   Send out a company-wide email retelling the story of the victory. Highlight it at a meeting. (Up the ante by creating a memorable physical totem or symbol of this victory, one that you can pass on to the next person to celebrate the next victory.)

   Gather everyone's attention in the office for a standing ovation (or bow down to the excellence that your team member showed— literally!)

   You get the idea—reinforce key behaviors that you want other people to internalize.

3. **Look for small stories that symbolize deeper meaning.**
   You don't need to highlight only victories. Instead, also look for small occurrences in the company that symbolize deeper values you want the company to absorb.

For example, if Carol came in on Saturday to double-check that the Acme redesign was still running smoothly, and you want that same degree of diligence and care to be core values, then publicly thank Carol for it. Ask her how it went and what she learned, and then share those insights again with your whole team (which lets you again subtly retell the underlying story of Carol caring enough to check on the redesign on Saturday).

4. **Intentionally make the hard decision that shocks your team into learning how seriously you believe in your values.**
   This might mean firing a key client who just doesn't fit with the direction and mission of the business. Or publicly accepting responsibility for a poor decision and cutting off a failed project. Your team needs to see you model and live your culture. They are watching very closely, even when you don't see them.

5. **Start from the point of recruitment—bring your values and culture front and center into your hiring, selection, and orientation of new team members.**
   Build into your hiring process checks for personality and values fit with your company's culture. Make sure when you bring on a new hire that explaining the company values isn't just a 10-minute talk, but it is something you communicate by having multiple people share stories and experiences to make those values and the culture real.

6. **If you want high performance and personal responsibility to be an integral part of your company culture, you've got to cull out your low performers—now!**
   Every company has them: those team members who everyone knows are just marking time and sliding by. If you give them a pass by not dealing with the situation, the message you're sending to the rest of your team is that poor performance and excuses are acceptable.

   High performers find a team with deadweight demotivating. Cull your lower performers now and replace them with better and better people. Yes, this might cause some short-term pain, but the long-term rewards merit it.

Remember, culture is what empowers your team to deal with novel situations that your systems and controls just don't cover.

#6: Strategic Structure—Your Regular Process for Guiding Your Company's Strategic Choices

How do you consistently get your company to invest its time, talent, attention, and money into the right things in the face of so many demands and urgencies crying out for its resources?

This is where your **strategic structure** comes into play.

At its most basic form, your strategic structure is how your business rationally and effectively plans its pathway forward as you scale. It includes your annual planning to set goals and create your map for the coming year, quarterly planning to check in on progress and gain clarity for the coming quarter's action plan, and weekly execution and accountability to follow your quarterly action plan and get the results you want.

Your annual planning includes you asking questions like:

1. **What business you are trying to build? Over the next three to five years, what is your number one business goal?** Too many business owners never stop and clarify in writing the business they are working so hard to create. What does your ideal business look like in three to five years? What does it look like quantitatively? (For example, what are its sales figures, its market share, its margins, the size of the average client, etc.?) What does it look like qualitatively? (For example, what is it known for? What niches does it focus on? Who are its best customers? What does the team look like? What is your personal role in the company?)

2. **Where do you currently stand in relation to your number one business goal?** In other words, you're looking to identify the gap. If you are working to build $15 million per year in sales volume in the next five years with an operating profit margin of 20 percent, where do you stand right now? What is the gap that you'll have to bridge between where you are today and where you want to get to in the future? In your annual strategic planning you'll create your written map to bridge (or at least narrow) this gap.

3. **What is your single biggest limiting factor inside your business?** In other words, what one limitation is currently doing the most to limit the growth and success of your business? Getting clear on your limiting factor is one of your top leverage points in- side your business. It is a great clue to where you should invest some of your top resources of time, attention, money, and talent to create a big result for your business.

4. **What are 10 or more potential ways to push back or make your limiting factor(s) less limiting for your business?** Again, this is a challenge worth solving. When you do solve it, you automatically grow your business in a leveraged way. So get your leadership team together and brainstorm as many ways as you can to push that limiting factor back or make it irrelevant.

5. **Go back through your list of 10 solutions; which of your potential ideas are low-hanging fruit?** Low-hanging fruit are solutions that are easy or straightforward to implement, and they have a high likelihood of working and of producing a result.

6. **Go back through your list of 10 solutions; which of your potential ideas are home runs?** A home run is a solution that *if* it works, the payoff is BIG!

7. **Which ideas are your sweet spots?** Going back to your list of 10 solutions to each of your limiting factors, circle the solutions that are *both* low-hanging fruit and home runs. These are your sweet spots. By definition these are the critical areas where you need to invest the best resources inside your business. They are easy to do, have a high likelihood of working, *and* have a BIG payoff.

Taking all of this into consideration, map out your year. What progress do you want to make toward your most important three- to five-year goal? What is your revenue goal for the coming year? Your profit target? Your other key performance indicator (KPI) goals that if you hit them will increase your odds of successfully making meaningful progress toward your one-year and three- to five-year goals? What is your strategy to reach these goals? What is your rough plan—quarter by quarter—to execute on your strategy and reach your objectives?

Armed with your annual map, next you'll need to create your quarterly plan of action. Why quarterly? Because the quarter is the perfect unit of time to bridge your big-picture goals, which likely have a two- to five-year timeline or longer, and your weekly planning and daily actions.

The quarter is the key to executing on your strategy to accomplish your business goals. It's long enough that you can get meaningful units of work done that collectively bring you closer to your long-term goals, but short enough so that you can frequently course correct and hold your focus.

For over a decade now we've pushed our business coaching clients to follow our **one-page plan of action**. You likely are asking why we have this strong bias for a one-page plan of action; why not two pages, or five, or 25 pages? *Why one page?*

Because we've learned from our work coaching thousands of companies that in the rush of the day to day, if your plan is two or three pages you just won't use it weekly to guide your execution of that plan. With a one-page plan you'll review it every week, and pull the needed action steps to add into your weekly execution system. Plus you'll be able to review your key leadership team's quarterly one-page action plan each week and quickly check in and hold them accountable for their behaviors, too. In essence your one-page plan of action becomes your quarterly and weekly GPS to make sure that your team is focusing on the right things, and hitting the key milestones on time.

In Figure 2.1 you can see what our formatted action plans look like. You can download a free PDF copy of this and many of our other strategic planning tools by going to **www.MauiMastermind.com/freetoolkit**. (See Appendix A for full details.)

Creating your one-page plan of action is a simple, three-step process:

Step One: Pick your top three Focus Areas for the quarter.

Your top Focus Areas are the three most important areas for your business to spotlight during the coming quarter.

SAMPLE QUARTERLY STRATEGIC ACTION PLAN

Focus Area One: Increasing production capacity **Criteria of Success:** • Written process for how we produce our core service. • Conducted a Sweet Spot Analysis to increase our production capacity by 15+%. • KPI: Revenue generated per service team production days.	Action Steps/Milestones	Who	By When
	☐ Map out our current "production" system. Identify biggest current constraints. Conduct Sweet Spot Analysis to best increase production capacity.	Carlos	1-15-xx
	☐ Review Sweet Spot ideas and pick the winners. Create implementation plan.	Carlos	1-31-xx
	☐ Formal check-in #1: Insights? What's working? What adjustments need to be made? Update plan.	Carlos	2-21-xx
	☐ Formal check-in #2: Insights? What's working? What adjustments need to be made? Update plan.	Carlos	3-15-xx
	☐ Review status at end of quarter—capture lessons and plan to refine production system into Version 2.0 next quarter.	Carlos	3-30-xx

Focus Area Two: Hire a great director of marketing **Criteria of Success:** • Have clear, written role and candidate descriptions. • Reduce candidate profile to the 5 "must haves" and hire to those specific items. • Have written onboarding plan to successfully integrate our new hire. • Formally debrief at end and improve our hiring process for future.	Action Steps/Milestones	Who	By When
	☐ Create a written job description and candidate profile. Reduce to the 5 "must haves" for this role. Review both with key stakeholders.	Tina	1-15-xx
	☐ Create our written recruitment game plan.	Tina	1-21-xx
	☐ Launch recruitment efforts.	Tina	1-31-xx
	☐ Run our selection process and get to our finalist candidates.	Tina	3-7-xx
	☐ Create our written onboarding plan for this hire.	Tina	3-15-xx
	☐ Hire our winning candidate and run our onboarding process.	Tina	3-30-xx
	☐ Formally debrief process: What worked best? What can we do to improve our hiring process for future? Update hiring process based on learnings.	Tina	3-30-xx

Focus Area Three: Increase client retention **Criteria of Success:** • Complete retention analysis and explicitly identify the 1–2 biggest "drop points." • Retention "Tiger Team" to conduct Sweet Spot Analysis and implement ideas to increase retention. • Formally debrief at end and create Q2 plan to continue improving retention rate. • KPI: Retention score.	Action Steps/Milestones	Who	By When
	☐ Analyze current retention stats and drop points. Share results with retention Tiger Team.	Marcus	1-15-xx
	☐ Conduct Sweet Spot Analysis to increase retention rate. Pick 1 or 2 winners and create implementation plan for quarter.	Marcus	1-21-xx
	☐ Formal check-in #1: Insights? What's working? What adjustments need to be made? Update plan.	Marcus	1-31-xx
	☐ Formal check-in #2: Insights? What's working? What adjustments need to be made? Update plan.	Marcus	3-7-xx
	☐ Share results with leadership team along with formal retention game plan for next quarter.	Marcus	3-15-xx

Figure 2.1: Format for One-Page Quarterly Plan of Action for Your Company

Sure, you'll still have to take care of the day-to-day operational needs of your business, but your Focus Areas are those areas you've identified where you will invest a portion of your best resources that quarter because you know that these areas are what will really help you scale and develop your business.

Potential Focus Areas could be:

- Increasing your lead flow.
- Improving your sales conversion system.
- Speeding up your collections cycle.
- Making a specific key hire.
- Developing a new product.
- Progressing on a key project.

We strongly advise you to limit your company to only three Focus Areas for the quarter as your top priorities. Why limit your company to three Focus Areas? Because 90 days pass quickly, and if you spread your company too thin, you'll find that you partially do more things instead of fully doing a few key chunks that actually produce value for your company. Remember, less can often be more, especially when it's what you actually get *done.*

Step Two: Clarify the criteria of success for each of your three Focus Areas.

Now that you've picked your three Focus Areas for the quarter, the temptation is to immediately go lay out your action steps in this area for the quarter. Don't.

Instead, pause and first clarify your criteria of success for each Focus Area. *What would you need to accomplish this quarter in this Focus Area in order for you to be successful? What will you see, or what could you observe having been completed, that would let you* know *you were successful in this Focus Area this quarter?* Your written criteria of success for each Focus Area gives you a clear yardstick against which to measure progress as you go. It paints a clear picture of what success in this Focus Area, this quarter, looks like.

In order to keep your plan of action to one page, pick three or four definite criteria of success for each Focus Areas, including one **key performance indicator** (KPI) to track for each Focus Area.

Now that you've got your written criteria of success before you, step three (writing out your action steps and milestones) will be easy. Most of your action steps are obvious in your criteria of success.

Step Three: Lay out your key action steps and milestones for the quarter.

The final step is to lay out the key action steps and milestones you need to take or reach to accomplish your criteria of success for each Focus Area over the coming quarter.

In order to keep your plan to one page, you'll likely break each Focus Area down into five to seven action steps and milestones.

While your plan must be detailed enough to guide your actions, it must not be so detailed that you feel overwhelmed or lose yourself in the minutiae.

For each action step, pick a specific team member to be ultimately responsible for executing the step by a definite date. While you can have multiple people contribute to a specific step or steps, you need to pick one person who is tasked with the responsibility and authority to get that step done and done well. We say that this person "owns" the task. This sense of ownership is critical to your success. It's hard to hold anyone accountable for missed milestones when it wasn't clear who was really responsible in the first place.

With this structure, the owner doesn't have to do all of the work herself—she just needs to be responsible for making sure that it gets done in the best way possible within the company.

Over time as you get fluent with this planning process, you'll create a *company* one-page quarterly plan of action, and have each of your key executives create their own department or *pillar* one-page quarterly plan of action. Their pillar plan of action (e.g., sales, operations, finance, etc.) will connect their top priorities as a department with the most important priorities and objectives of the company. This coordinates and aligns all their efforts to get an enhanced result (see "#7: Coherence").

The final element of your strategic structure is your weekly accountability and execution. While we recommend the quarter as the unit to connect your big-picture goals and objectives to the practical level of execution, we recommend that you use the *week* as your basic unit to connect execution to practical, in-the-trenches, behavioral doing, day in, day out.

We've developed a tool to help you execute weekly called "The Big Rock Report." Essentially, the way this tool works is that at the start of each week, you and your key staff each pick two or three "Big Rocks." Big Rocks are specific action steps, tasks, or chunks of a key project that if you did them in the coming week would do the most to progress your business toward its most important goals. Why do we call them Big

Rocks? Because these are the big things from which you build your success, week by week, quarter by quarter, year by year.

Each Big Rock should be something that takes no more than two hours. If it is likely to take longer, then break it down into smaller bite-sized chunks. Why two hours or less? Because even following the time mastery strategies you'll learn about in Chapter 5 it's unlikely you'll be consistently able to block off a bigger chunk of time. By keeping your Big Rocks to steps you can take and complete in a one- to two-hour chunk or less, you'll increase your odds of getting them done.

So the first part of your weekly "Big Rock Report" is to review how you did on your prior week's Big Rocks. Did you get them all done? What were the outcomes? What did you learn? Are any next steps still needed? What other information would you want to share with your team on this item?

Then you list out your Big Rocks for the coming week. Review your one-page action plan. What steps do you need to take this coming week to keep yourself on target to meet or exceed your quarterly plan of action?

#7: Coherence—Aligning Your Goals, Priorities, Actions, and Team

What if there were a magic concept that you could employ that would powerfully align your company's goals, priorities, actions, and culture?

In other words, your company would invest its best resources in alignment with its top goals. And each member of your team would act daily in accordance with these priorities, letting these priorities and agreed-upon objectives guide their actions and execution. And finally, as a company, you'd hold to this discipline long enough so that this pattern of behavior would become the norm for your company.

Well, there is just such a magic concept, and it's called "coherence." Coherence is a term from physics that refers to light rays being in sync with each other—strengthening and reinforcing each other.

In the context of your business, **coherence means the core parts of your business all being aligned and in sync with one another, supporting and reinforcing each other**.

Too many companies have great goals on paper, but simply don't act in alignment with those goals or with their stated priorities and values. Instead, these underperforming companies allow their efforts to become fractured and scattered, often working counter to each other.

The most successful companies get all their moving parts working in alignment with each other to achieve their top objectives in a manner consistent with their core values and priorities.

While this is a simple concept to understand in theory, it is a difficult one to apply in practice.

Here are 10 tips to help you bring your company's goals, priorities, actions, and culture into coherence:

1. **Get clear on your goals and priorities.** As obvious as it sounds, many companies perform poorly and are scattered simply because they don't have clear goals and priorities.

2. **Propagate your goals and priorities throughout your organization.** It's not enough to have goals and priorities; you've got to make sure your team knows, understands, and buys into them.

3. **Spot-check to see if your team really understands your goals and priorities.** Ask them, *"What do you see as our company's top three goals?"* If you discover, as you likely will, that what you thought was simple and clear was neither, use this as an opportunity to coach and redirect.

4. **Help your team connect their department and individual goals and priorities to the company's.** It's great to have three top goals as a company, but what does that mean to your operations manager? How about to your accounting department? And your sales team? You've got to make sure that you bring your goals and priorities into context for each of your team members and departments.

5. **Translate your team member and department goals and priorities into observable behaviors and concrete action steps.** How will they know they are operating in alignment with your company's goals and priorities? What will they *do* over the next 90 days—behaviorally—that will progress the company in alignment with these goals and priorities? You've got to make it concrete and *behavioral.*

6. **Get your management team to review company and department behavior at least monthly (ideally biweekly) to make sure it is in alignment with company goals and priorities.** If it isn't (which is likely to be the case initially), use this as an opportunity to coach and redirect.

7. **Accept that, for most companies, this is going to be a long, slow process of applying gentle pressure—relentlessly.** Over time, you will be able to shape the behaviors and norms for your company so that this aligned behavior becomes part of your company culture.

8. **Highlight stories and successes of how individuals, teams, departments, or the company as a whole acted in alignment with its goals and priorities.** Shaping culture requires lots of small nudges. Look for any reasonable excuse to give things one more nudge.

9. **Role model the behavior you want your team to internalize.** If you aren't consistent with what you're asking team members to do, they'll spot it in an instant and you'll lose all credibility.

10. **Use tough, emotional moments as examples of how serious your company is about living its goals and priorities.** A tough decision in alignment with your company values and priorities will have more impact on your real culture than any dozen easy moves you make.

Is all of this easy? No. Is it worthwhile? You bet it is.

#8: Accountability—Creating a Culture of Meeting Commitments and Keeping Promises

Great businesses are built on teams that take full ownership of individual responsibilities. Too many businesses let people slide by partially doing things and accepting excuses for delays and mistakes that could have been avoided. A culture of accountability is one of the most valuable institutional habits that your business can form, and, for better or worse, it starts with you. If you don't move heaven and earth to honor your word and meet all your commitments, your team will learn that they don't have to, either.

Here are seven time-tested tips on your role in creating accountability in your company:

1. **Clarify your commitments in writing at the end of every meeting.** Not only does this ensure that you've captured all your action items, but it is also a powerful way to role model how you want your team to behave.

   Wherever possible, try to enumerate all your commitments to make it even clearer what you have agreed you'll do.

For example, this might look like, *"So, summing up, I've got three action items here. Item one…item two…and item three…"* [Visibly writing each of them down in your notes.]

When your team sees you consistently sum up and write down action steps and who owns them (and by when) after every meeting you'll be amazed at how quickly they will raise their game and start to follow the same behavior. Plus, this will make it worlds easier for you to remember to circle back and check with your team that they have met their commitments and to close the loop by telling them how you met the commitments you made yourself to them at the meeting. Which brings us to the next tip:

2. **Circle back with the team members who are involved with your action steps, and give them feedback on your progress and completion at regular intervals.**

   This is a great way to role model the behavior you want from them, and to highlight how important it is inside your company to meet deliverables.

   This might sound like, *"Just wanted to give you a quick update. As committed to, I did* [item one] *and* [item two] *today, and will get* [item three] *done by close of business Friday."*

   Even when the task isn't complete, don't leave people guessing.

   Circle back and say, *"I haven't solved the problem yet, but I haven't forgotten you and I'm actively working on a solution."* Again, you are modeling to your team the behavior of taking full responsibility.

3. **Clearly state what you can't commit to so that you don't lower the accountability bar in your company through missing a "phantom deliverable."**

   Beware of phantom deliverables—the things that the other person *thinks* you committed to but you didn't.

   As a leader, you need to model great communication by making explicit any phantom deliverables you see come out of a meeting. That way if you can commit to that deliverable, you do so, and if you can't, you clarify that you are not committing to it.

4. **Be on time, all the time.**

   It may not seem like it matters, but it does.

   Being on time—all the time—is a simple behavior that your team will generalize to mean that you take your commitments seriously and live in integrity.

It is one behavior with a huge return on investment in terms of modeling accountability inside your company.

Too many companies implement respect in a hierarchical manner. Your time is not more important than an employee's time or a customer's time in their eyes.

Being on time shows respect, and it makes a big difference to the receiver.

A corollary of this is to start your meetings on time, versus waiting for the late arrivals to saunter in. You'd better believe they'll get the message that integrity matters when they come into the meeting six minutes late and you take them aside afterward to ask them why they were late.

5. **Stay the course—credibility is a marathon, not a sprint.**
It doesn't help if you take off out of the gate gung ho in your desire to model accountability, only to let it slip a few weeks later. How you model accountability is a key ingredient in building your company culture.

If you want it to be real and lasting, you've got to maintain your behavior over time.

6. **Take responsibility for your mistakes—how you own your mistakes and failures is as important as how you model your successes.**
You're human—we all are—so you *will* mess up. Of course you will, and to think otherwise is just not realistic.

How you own your missed deliverables is incredibly important to the culture you are building. Do you make excuses? Sweep them under the rug? Melodramatically beat yourself up?

Instead, we encourage you to show your team how mistakes are a part of being in business, and often can lead to profitable insights.

When you make a mistake, publicly take responsibility, share what you learned and how you'll apply it, and implement a better solution going forward.

7. **Hand off smoothly and completely—most breakdowns in accountability come from incomplete or poor handoffs.**
At the moment any deliverable is created, it needs to get assigned to someone who will be responsible to see that it happens. We call this assignment of a deliverable a handoff.

As a leader, you need to model that every handoff clearly details who is responsible for what and by when, what success in meeting that deliverable looks like, and how he or she will be held accountable for that deliverable. (Think back to the first tip.)

"Sarah, you own this deliverable and it includes doing X and Y by close of business Friday. Can you also please make sure to send a quick recap to Tom and me on Monday that shares how Client Z responded?"

The combination of these seven time-tested tips, applied with gentle pressure—relentlessly—will have a big impact inside your company in shaping your team to help your business achieve and sustain growth.

Here is one more secret to leverage the power of accountability to successfully build an owner-independent company.

Leverage a Business Coach to Hold You Accountable and Accelerate Your Progress

A business coach is an experienced entrepreneur who's been where you want to go and can give you the outside perspective and counsel to build a more successful business—without having to go through all the painful trial and error yourself. Just like a coach does for a sports team, a business coach's role is to help your company focus, plan, execute, and regroup so that you make consistent progress growing your business and building an owner-independent company.

Too many business owners build their businesses in isolation, lacking the outside perspective and feedback from an experienced mentor. What's more, most business owners don't have anyone in their business lives to challenge their thinking and to question their assumptions. Sure, you may have lots of employees, but it's asking a lot for an employee who depends on you for his or her family's financial support to really challenge you with the things you don't want to hear but desperately need to hear.

David's friend and coauthor of SCALE, Jeff Hoffman (cofounder of Priceline.com), put it this way: *"What I get out of having a business coach is that my coach has run and worked with so many companies that he's seen almost every situation. So when I don't even know how to handle a new situation, my coach says, 'Don't worry about it. I've seen this pattern a dozen times. Here's how to best handle it.'"*

Here are our top tips to get the most out of your business coach:

- **Pick a coach who has a deep experience set and knowledge base to draw upon.** The whole idea of leveraging a business coach is to help you avoid a lot of the expensive trial and error that most business owners take as they build a business. While many of the situations you come up against in your business (whether they be about managing your team, growing your sales, creating your next products or services, or controlling your expenses) may be new to you, your coach can draw on his or her past experiences to give you clarity on the best path forward.

- **Pick a coach who can articulate and explain things to you in simple, step-by-step language so that you can integrate what the coach shares and put it to immediate and effective use.**

- **Meet frequently with your business coach—but not *too* often.** We recommend every two weeks as the optimal interval. This is often enough that you get effective accountability (monthly is generally not often enough for this), but not so often that you don't have time to get things done.

- **Give your business coach weekly updates on your progress.** Five to 15 minutes spent each week to update your coach about your progress both adds a layer of accountability into the mix and keeps your coach up to speed with your company so he can give you his best input. David's business coaching clients use his company's "Big Rock App" each week to automatically update the business coach on their progress for the prior week.

- **Share your numbers—candidly.** Yes, it can be scary to share your revenue, gross margin, and operating profit figures with complete candor, but by being open you will get valuable outside perspective and feedback. Don't sugarcoat *anything*. Your coach won't judge you. Her real desire is to help you grow and succeed, and to do that she needs accurate data.

- **Don't just focus on one-off challenges—look for systematic, global solutions.** Solving a challenge is great, but solving a challenge in a way that improves and develops your company's internal systems and controls is even more valuable. Ad hoc solutions are hard to scale. Systems-driven solutions are more stable and easier to grow.

- **Pick a program, not just a coach.** You want and need more than just a great coach; you want a solid, proven coaching *program*. Remember, structure plus talent always outperforms talent isolated on its own. In effect, the right coaching *program* makes sure that your coach balances your company's immediate day-to-day operational needs with its longer-term development strategy. If your coach just helps you deal with your current operational challenges but doesn't give you a clear map to consistently reduce your company's reliance on you by enhancing its systems, team, controls, and culture, you just may end up more firmly trapped in an owner-reliant Level Two business.

- **Give permission to your business coach to hold you accountable**. The right business coach will always be in your corner, and sometimes this means being the one person in your business life who calls you on the mat. Your employees can't do this—you sign their paychecks.

- **Don't rationalize or explain away reality, because even if you win the discussion, reality will still win the war.** We both smile when we think about all the exceptionally smart and articulate business owners we've known over the years who at one point or another thought they could explain away a challenge or situation with a well-rehearsed argument. Reality is what reality is, and the objective facts are the objective facts. Your coach will help you cut through your own rationalizations and fantasy thinking, helping you take full responsibility and accept the objective facts on the ground. And from this place you can together come up with an effective plan of action to harness those facts to reach your business goals.

- **Let down your ego and accept the help and insights of your business coach.** You don't have to posture or look good. Your coach has seen just about everything you are dealing with and has worked through it. Let your coach save you time, energy, emotion, and money by helping you learn from his or her experiences versus painful and expensive trial and error.

- **Get rid of your excuses.** You don't have to do it perfectly, but you do have to take action. Of course you're busy, but when will that ever really change if you don't do the things that reduce your company's reliance on you? If you want to enjoy the growth and freedom that the right business coach can help you achieve, then you've got to let go of your excuses and dive fully into the commitment. Sure, you'll mess up and have setbacks, but we've seen the magic that can happen over 36 months or longer of focused, directed, intelligent action in scaling a company. Time's going to pass either way. What will you be saying three years from today? *"If only I had . . ."* or *"I'm so glad I did!"*? So dive in and put your coach's input into action.

When we spoke with Shirley about her experiences working with her business coach to help her scale her schools, here's what she shared. *"One of my biggest breakthroughs came when I was talking with my business coach Patty and she challenged me in a new way about why I felt like no one else could do the things I was doing as well as they needed to be done. Patty had me take a close look at the price I was paying in my life by holding on to that limiting belief. It wasn't easy, and I still struggle with letting go to my management team, but the key difference is that now I have not only started to build a capable and talented management team, but have delegated responsibility for the administrative functions to others. Additionally, I have learned to not settle for sub-standard performance from my managers and have hired capable directors and assistant directors at both schools who can handle almost every issue."*

Beware the Naysayers

While all this talk about scaling your business to an owner-independent Level Three company sounds great in theory, we know the world is full of naysayers who will tell you it can't be done. They'll say that the only way to build a business is through hard work and long hours. They'll tell you it just isn't possible for you to build a Level Three business. (Ironically, many of these naysayers are people who actually work for Level Three businesses! But hey, why should that stop them from preaching doom and gloom?)

Well, we got tired of hearing all the naysayers in the world, so we initiated a national business search to select a business owner we would work with for 120 days and *prove* it was possible to take a business to the next level in an incredibly short period of time. We joined forces with companies like Dun & Bradstreet, Hoovers, Comcast, and AllBusiness.com to promote our search, and after an exhaustive selection process we winnowed down the 1,000-plus applicants to 14 finalists. Their businesses were as diverse as a consulting business, manufacturing company, construction firm, collections agency, professional services firm, lifestyle company, and cruise line. In the end, we chose a small niche software company located in Arizona owned by Jennifer Lyle.

Jennifer had taken over the software company after buying out two partners a few years before our challenge began. At that time, the business had stagnated as the typical owner-reliant Level Two business. Jennifer ran all the sales, managed all the staff, made all the key decisions, and put out all the important fires. She just didn't know that her business could be any other way. She put in intense hours to make it work and had a deep commitment to succeed, which is why the editors of AllBusiness.com selected her as the contest grand prize winner.

How would you like to have five of the world's top entrepreneurs select you and your business to work hand in hand with for an intense period to take your business to the next level? Well, that's exactly what we did with Jennifer. We helped her map out her business growth strategy. We helped her retool her sales team and define her sales offer. We helped her create her hiring plan. We held her accountable for how she spent her time so she did the things that would make the biggest difference for her business in the shortest amount of time.

The results? They speak for themselves. Within six months, Jennifer's sales were up more than 80 percent and her profitability had jumped an impressive 150 percent.

Today, seven years after that original contest, Jennifer has continued to work with David's company and grow her company. *"Last year my business generated 9 times the operating profit than it did since the contest,"* Jennifer shared in a recent email to David. *"I have more time off, am more relaxed, and have a much better quality of life."*

But alas, despite the stellar results of this challenge, the naysayers of the world will still say it can't be done. They'll give you all sorts of reasons why you can't do this or shouldn't do that. And if you listen to them, what results are you guaranteed to get? The exact same results you're getting right now. *Nothing will change unless you commit and take action to make it change.*

If you can tune out the naysayers or, better yet, transform their input into an incentive to prove them wrong and aggressively grow your business, you're destined to take your business to the next level faster than you could imagine.

Whenever we're working with a business owner, we're always working toward that magic day when she finally "gets it" that she can have her business *and* have her life outside of it. Yes, it's possible. When you build your business the right way, you get both the money and the freedom.

Speaking of naysayers, if we're really being honest with ourselves, we are usually our own biggest critics. That was true for one of our clients, Marichiel. Before we met her she was the typical owner-reliant business owner, running her real estate appraisal company. One of her very close friends was a client of ours who went on to found and scale a wildly successful health business. Marichiel watched her friend succeed but kept telling herself she couldn't do it. That was until she suffered a family tragedy that shook her world. In a miraculous way, Marichiel came out of the sadness stronger and committed to be an example for her young son. She took a leap of faith and resolved to build a different outcome for herself and her family.

It was hard work in the beginning, but Marichiel was determined to succeed. She connected with an upgraded peer group of business owners, listened to our coaching, and followed the Level Three Map to build her company the right way. Within three years she had matured the company to the point where she was working less than five hours a week, the company was flourishing, and she had the time to start a second business.

Marichiel is a great example of what is truly possible if you can face down your inner naysayer. Here's how she expressed herself in a letter she sent to us:

> *"Not only do I have what you taught me, but so do my children and future generations to come. I am creating a legacy because of you. Thank you for creating Maui Mastermind."*

In the next chapter, we'll dive deep into the Level Three Map and lay out the entire life cycle of your business from launch to exit. Plus you'll learn why your owner-independent Level Three company will be worth 10 times its owner-reliant Level Two counterpart.

CHAPTER 3

The Level Three
Map in Detail

Brian grew up in the family business. His dad, Ronnie, started the manufacturing firm; his mom, Marge, ran many of the administrative and financial aspects of the company; and family life revolved around the company.

Brian studied engineering and earned his degree. After college he came back home and went to work for the family business, quickly proving to be one of its most talented engineers. With Ronnie's tight grip on the company and Marge to back him up, the company grew sales to more than $15 million per year. And then tragedy struck. Brian's dad died.

It was then, with no leadership team in place and a culture that had learned to lean heavily on Ronnie for key decisions, that the company was at real risk of failure. Brian was a great engineer, but with the loss of his father he was pushed into the role of running the whole company, something for which he wasn't fully ready.

Brian considered selling the company for his mom. He didn't want to do anything wrong that might jeopardize her future. But he also believed in the business, and felt that with a better map, he could lead it through this critical transition.

This was when Brian attended one of David's business conferences. When Brian went through the Level Three Map he immediately understood what had happened to his father's manufacturing company. Ronnie had built an owner-reliant "Middle Stage" Level Two business. Brian realized that while the company had solid production systems in place, it lacked a management team, strategic map, and coherent process to guide its growth. Ronnie had just kept all of these things in his head, and now, without him, the company was struggling.

The first step Brian took after joining the business coaching program was to take stock of what was and was not working—pillar by pillar—in- side the company. This detailed audit became the base for a strategic plan to save the business. That was the start of six years of hard, diligent work to grow the company, to mature its internal functioning, to develop a leadership team, and to integrate a quarterly strategic process that kept the company investing its best resources in its best opportunities. And the work paid off—handsomely. Under Brian's leadership, the company quadrupled its operating profit and built a much stronger base to ensure its future. Along the way Brian and his company progressed through the steps and stages of the Level Three Map.

Let's take another pass through the Level Three Map, going into detail and breaking down Level Two into three distinct stages: Early, Middle, and Advanced. At each stage, your Level Two business will have different characteristics and specific needs. You'll find that understanding this detailed view of the Level Three Map will get you locked on course and focused on the right outcomes for your specific level and stage. In the end, this will shave years off your journey to Level Three. (See Figure 3.1.)

Level One: Planning Your Business and Proving It's Viable

At Level One, you're designing and planning your new start-up. You're gathering your initial team, raising any required start-up capital, and executing your launch plan. Your focus at Level One is to plan your new

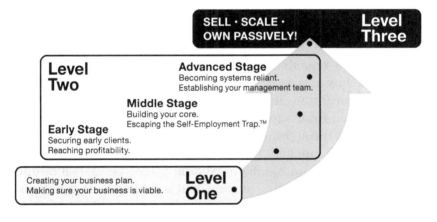

Figure 3.1: Level Three Map™
Copyright © Maui Mastermind®

business and get immediate market feedback to learn if your business concept and model are economically viable. This is a fancy way of saying you'll be testing your product or service to see if you can sell it at a price that allows your business to be profitable.

Because the focus of this book is on helping you take your existing business into a thriving, owner-independent Level Three company, we won't be spending any time with Level One start-ups in this book. Once you've drafted a business plan and gotten direct market feedback to prove that it's viable, it's time to move to Level Two Early Stage.

Level Two Early Stage: Making Your Business Sustainable

Focus: Securing your early clients and becoming profitable.
Leverage Points: Your ability to change and adapt, keeping costs low and your business lean.

Fresh in the marketplace, an Early Stage Level Two business has just started actively marketing and selling its products/services. This is the time to learn your business and market and, if needed, discover and cure any potentially fatal flaws in your business model or in the way your targeted customers perceive the value you're creating.

Your early focus while launching a business isn't on building the perfect product or service, but rather on figuring out how you can get people to buy. Too many entrepreneurs get caught in the trap of making the perfect gizmo, but never actually *sell that gizmo in large enough numbers* to ensure a profit.

Know that at this stage in your business's growth, you'll be wearing just about every hat in the business. That's okay for now, but as you move toward Middle Stage Level Two, you'll need to find ways to leverage your personal production for the business by hiring staff and building basic business systems.

Remember, an Early Stage Level Two business is working to generate sales, establish a market position, and become a sustainable business.

Priority #1: Sell, Sell, Sell!

Focus initially on your sales and marketing efforts—it's critical! If you can't sell your product or service, you don't have a sustainable business. So pull out your business plan and start executing the marketing and sales plan you laid out in your business plan draft.

Create your "top prospect list" and start making sales calls. (Alternatively, if your marketing plan calls for selling via channel partners or joint venture partners, then get to work calling on them.)

Who are your top 25 prospective customers or joint venture/channel partners? Listing what you know about your top prospects helps you gather information that leads to those all-important early sales. So start a file on each of them and include the following information:

1. Why is this customer such a great client/partner lead?

2. Why is your business a great fit for what this customer needs?

3. Who do you know inside those organizations? Who could personally introduce you to these people or organizations, whether they're insiders or not?

4. Who are the decision makers? If you're selling directly to consumers, how, when, and where do they normally make their buying decisions on your product/service? How do you get in front of those decision makers?

Execute your marketing plan. This might call for you to:

- sell at a trade show or at local markets.

- rent direct mail lists of prospects to mail and call.

- network for leads at your local chamber of commerce and other groups.

- buy key word advertising to generate traffic to your website.

- actively post to discussion forums and blogs to spread the word about your business.

- use social media (Facebook, Twitter, LinkedIn, etc.) to get the word out.

At this juncture, it's essential that you secure an adequate lead flow so you not only generate the sales needed to become profitable, but you can also develop your base sales and marketing system.

To create a successful business requires more than just making a sale here or there. You've got to build the business in a way that will reliably generate ongoing sales. You need this dependable stream of sales in order to build the baseline marketing and sales system that you can later scale.

Take the case of John, a business owner who came to us with a difficult dilemma. His new teleconference company was an Early Stage Level

Two business with sales that covered about 70 percent of its costs. He had an exciting opportunity to change the company's business model for the better, yet had reached a crossroads and knew it. He wanted our input to help him make a pivotal decision either to shift focus to this new venture or to stay with his original business model.

Too many business owners make poor and costly decisions simply because they're too close to their businesses and don't have the perspective they need to see things accurately. That's a huge benefit of having outside peers and advisors you can turn to in order to provide this perspective. That's also why we think it's difficult and dangerous to build your business in isolation.

First, we asked John objective questions so we could accurately view his situation and desired outcome, and then determine his realistic options. After going through our question sequence, three things became clear to John. First, his new business model was unproven and hence a gamble, but also one with a big upside if successful. In fact, if it worked, he would be creating a brand-new market that his business could dominate. Second, his current business efforts were working; conservatively, the business was five months away from becoming profitable. Third, once the business reached profitability under his existing business plan, it would be fairly straightforward to maintain and incrementally grow the current sales volume.

Once these key data points were laid out, his decision became easy. John chose to aggressively focus on reaching profitability under his existing business plan. This would give him the financial strength and sustainability he needed to take a chance and refocus some of his best talent on establishing this new market while developing his new business model.

When faced with a tough business decision that has serious consequences, we suggest getting structured, outside input to help clarify the current situation, your desired outcome, and your potential options. This is when you lean on your peers and advisors to help you think through your situation and the best choices. It's too easy to get locked into a stunted perspective. Besides, building any business in isolation is expensive, painful, and inefficient. We all need peers and advisors in our lives—people we can turn to and trust with tough decisions.

Priority #2: Start Creating Simple Systems and Structure to Operate Your Business

Remember, you aren't building permanent systems yet; rather, you're building initial processes by which you can effectively sell and then fulfill on your promises to customers and clients. Once you have enough sales coming in to validate your business, make sure you balance your time between generating more sales and building the internal structure of your business.

STEPHANIE'S STORY

When we originally took over Pacific Plastics and Engineering, the old owner had no formal business systems in place. We quickly learned that our customers were fed up with the long history of broken promises that the old owner had made but not honored. One of the first things we did was visit each of the customers. We sat down and talked with them to learn what they felt our business had promised them. Needing a way to capture and organize those promises, we laid them all out in a spreadsheet. The spreadsheet listed orders, delivery dates, and pricing information. This was one of our earliest business systems. Later, we expanded our systems to include an actual production manual for each of our manufacturing orders.

Now, years later, the company has a comprehensive and formal enterprise resource planning system that lays out each step in the process: quoting and pricing of new projects, automatic scheduling of incoming orders, engineering and machine setup, large-scale production, on-time delivery of all customer orders, and input into the financial system.

The systems it uses today took several years to develop and weren't something we could have laid out at the start of our business. We didn't know enough; the business wasn't developed enough. It's an iterative process wherein you start with the best system you can create, and over time you continually refine and redesign all your systems.

So start where your business is today and build a few rough systems to guide your work. You'll get more consistent results with less time, effort, and expense. Later, you can expand and upgrade your systems, but don't wait to start creating systems until you have the time and expertise to get them all done. Add one system at a time as you can. Take the first step now!

You'll find plenty of time to develop articulated business systems later. For now, make sure your business can survive, which means selling and delivering on your promises to customers and clients. At first, this can be as simple as creating an order form for taking phone orders, composing a checklist for all the deliverables due to your clients, or setting up an autoresponder email that thanks all new customers for their online orders. Later, this might mean creating an online project management system for doing a trade show, setting up a company database (most likely hiring it out), or creating a work-flow process that details how you work with a new client.

You won't ever have time to sit down and write out all your business systems in one fell swoop. This is not only an unreasonable fantasy; it would actually be quite dangerous. Why? For three reasons.

First, at this stage, you are needed to both generate sales and handle part, if not all, of the operational side of your business. If you stop all this to exclusively create systems, your business will die. Think of it like your beating heart. Just as your body needs blood circulating, your business needs sales and cash flow. The key is to build your systems and infrastructure *while* maintaining your focus on generating sales and fulfilling your client promises.

Second, you don't yet have the experience to build out all your systems successfully. You have so much to learn from the practical experiences of growing your business. Regard building systems as an iterative process— one you simply do bit by bit.

Third, if you try to step away from the business and complete your business systems in one sitting, you'll end up force-feeding your team mandatory systems that you created without getting their input or meaningfully engaging your team in this process. If you've ever had kids, you realize that the best way to get your kids to eat healthy foods is to involve them in cooking the meals. The same goes with your staff. If you want your team to use, refine, and live your systems, you've got to get their involvement in creating them along the way.

Priority #3: When Your Business Can Afford It, Begin to Build Your Team

In most cases, your early hires will be employees or outsourced service providers you can use to leverage your time as the key producer for your business. Building your team might include:

- hiring on more office staff,
- recruiting a part-time salesperson, and/or
- outsourcing financial record keeping to a bookkeeper.

As you bring on new team members, take the opportunity to create the system for how to do each specific job. There won't be a better time than when you place a new person in the role. Then enlist each new hire in creating a rough system for how someone else in the role could best perform it.

Word of caution: Don't hire all at once. Rather, hire as you need to, making sure your business has the cash flow to afford the help. Remember, it also takes time for your business to absorb and integrate any of your new hires, especially if they are playing a big role in the business.

The goal of Early Stage Level Two is to create a sustainable business. When you've achieved this, then it's time to move to Level Two Middle Stage.

Level Two Middle Stage: Establishing Your Business Core

Focus: Establishing your business's foundation; building your business's core systems and structure

Key Leverage Point: Leveraging your time so you can invest at least 20 percent (one day a week) to building your business's core

Characteristics of a Typical Middle Stage Level Two Business:

- The business revolves around the owner. It is owner reliant.

- The owner must show up each day or the business suffers from the absence.

- The owner hits a revenue plateau; he or she can't work any harder or put in any more hours. The company is stuck.

- The outside world—especially customers—identifies the business with the owner and wants him or her to personally handle their transaction, project, or business relationship, which makes it even harder for the company to escape the Self-Employment Trap.

Most businesses get stuck in Middle Stage Level Two. Why? Because the owners build their businesses for control based primarily on their personal production. They are the ones who make the key decisions, close the big sales, and manage much of the day-to-day operations. Sadly, these typical Middle Stage Level Two business owners stay stuck at the tactical level of doing the job of the business instead of creating the time and space to step back and *build the business as a business.*

Middle Stage Level Two requires building your core systems, team, and controls while balancing your business's need for you to continue to lead its daily operation. This is a delicate balance between operating the business in the here and now and building the structure you'll need to grow beyond your current situation. Thankfully, you don't have to figure all this out yourself.

A Middle Stage Level Two must build out the baseline systems for its four core functions:

1. **Lead generation:** your system for finding prospects.

2. **Lead conversion:** your system for closing sales.

3. **Production and delivery:** your system for producing and fulfilling your core product or service.

4. **Collections:** your system for collecting on what you are owed.

These four systems—for finding leads, closing sales, producing your product or service, and collecting on your receivables—are the four core systems of every business.

As you learned in the preceding chapter, the average small-business owner gets trapped at Middle Stage Level Two inside the Self-Employment Trap. But not you. Instead, you can follow the Level Three Map and use this stage as a launching pad to start scaling your business.

The first key step for you to take if you are at this stage on the Level Three Map is to make building an owner-independent Level Three business a stated goal of your company. Share this goal with your team. When they understand how building an owner-independent company makes them more secure, increases their opportunities to contribute and earn, and helps them be part of a vibrant, growing company, they'll get on board and help you successfully make this journey.

But it all starts with your decision to make progressing to Level Three in your business a defined goal of your company. When you do, changes can happen very fast.

Take the case of Lainy Vanderway, who, along with her husband Wayne, was a finalist in our national business search mentioned earlier. She and Wayne had built a highly successful heavy manufacturing business in Oregon, but their company strictly revolved around the two of them. She ran the operations and financial areas of the business while Wayne ran the sales and marketing end.

In a way, Lainy and Wayne suffered from the curse of competency that hurts many capable entrepreneurs. They were smart, driven, and incredibly talented at doing the work of the business. They also were particular about how they wanted things to be done. This combination of factors lured them into building their business around themselves, which, as you learned, leads to the Self-Employment Trap.

They wanted a way out from the day-to-day operations of their business, a way that would allow them to also scale the company. After joining David's business coaching program, they made building an owner-independent business a stated goal of their company. Within their first year of the program they had grown the business to Advanced Stage Level Two. They had hired their first executive leader, a chief financial officer (CFO), to run the financial side of the business and provide a balanced voice to help them make better leadership decisions. They had implemented systems that got them out of much of the day-to-day operations. Their sales were up, and the company even expanded to a second manufacturing facility on the East Coast. Best of all, they expanded their discretionary time by 15 hours a week, allowing them to reinvest this time in scaling the company. The key lesson here is how fast change can happen when you make the clear commitment to have building an owner-independent company a stated goal of your business.

As a Middle Stage Level Two business owner, you're scrambling to do two things: (1) bring organization to the chaotic world of your developing business, and (2) impose this order in a way that enhances your sales.

Once you build out your core as described in Middle Stage Level Two, you'll progress to Advanced Stage Level Two and begin the important work of refining your systems, building your management team, and scaling your business in earnest.

Level Two Advanced Stage: Building a Systems-Reliant Company with a Winning Management Team

Focus: Increasing your capacity and scaling your business
Key Leverage Point: Your key team members' time, talent, skills, and focus

Characteristics of a Typical Advanced Stage Level Two Business:

As you begin to transition into Advanced Stage Level Two, your business will commonly have the following characteristics, which become your starting point:

- It's becoming more and more systems driven. (At least one or two of the five main areas of your business are managed by people other than you.)

- Your revenue is starting to climb.
- Your business may feel like it's bursting at the seams.

At Advanced Stage Level Two, you'll begin the important work of refining your systems, building your management team, and scaling your business in earnest. This is the "rapid growth" stage of your business.

In this stage you'll also begin to build out the auxiliary systems you need in other parts of your company, from hiring to training to marketing to managing and more. You'll see that your revenue is exploding, and often you'll feel like your business is bursting at the seams as you struggle to keep up with the growth.

A key shift at this stage is to enroll your team in building the systems, controls, and scalable solutions your business needs alongside you. Whereas a Middle Stage Level Two business owner commonly sees her team as a way to leverage her own personal production, an Advanced Stage Level Two business owner sees her team as partners in taking the business to the next level. This essential shift is what allows businesses to successfully make the leap to Level Three. As management guru Peter Drucker once said, *"The founder has to learn to become the leader of a team rather than a 'star' with 'helpers.'"*

Ron owned a $12 million per year manufacturing company making industrial control parts to automate manufacturing processes. His company was an industry leader with a 25-year history that was started out of Ron's home. But for Ron to grow his company and set it up to succeed past his active participation he knew that he needed to build a leadership team. This is when he first came to David's company seeking help. What Ron quickly came to realize was that he had a very competent group of team members, but he had always kept them compartmentalized, working on just their one aspect of the business. Within the first six months in the program, Ron started formalizing the company's goals and created a formal strategic structure to guide the company quarter by quarter. What's more, simply by bringing his department heads together to form his leadership team, the process of guiding the company quarter by quarter broke through the compartmentalized barriers they had struggled with previously. He gave them a voice in planning, problem solving, and leading the company. The results have been nothing short of revolutionary. Ron's company is on pace to more than double its operating profit over the coming 36 months.

An essential piece in building a Level Three business is enrolling your team in building the systems, controls, and scalable solutions with you. Rather than regarding the team around you as a form of leverage that magnifies your personal reach and production, instead see them as partners in taking the business to the next level. So build up your team; let them shine. You don't need to be the one who has the best ideas or who gets the credit or plum assignments. Let your team step center stage, and start to shift your role to that of support player and stage manager.

Reaching Level Three requires finding and enlisting key members to "own" parts of your business. More important, it requires you to let go of control so your business can thrive without you.

Rather than have all roads lead back to and through you like a hub in the center of a wheel, encourage your team to work with one another directly. Grow their capacity to make their own decisions and take the initiative within the company. Remember, a business dependent on its owner—you—for its success becomes a prison that traps you. Plan for your great prison escape now by building your management team. Before long, you'll have key leaders in each of the five core pillars of your business: sales/marketing, operations, team, finance, and executive leadership.

In addition, make sure that your leaders and team members have a unified vision of what the business is, where it's heading, and how you plan to get there. This lets you set clear priorities, assign responsibilities, and hold each other accountable for results.

Criteria That Determine When You've Reached Level Three

What exactly does it look like when you've reached Level Three? First, you'll have solid leaders in place in four of the five core areas of your business. Yes, you may still hold on to the role of CEO for a while, provided you still enjoy a daily involvement leading the business. But you have the strategy, systems, and traditions in place to hire a new CEO if you choose. That means your business would thrive even if you were there only two or three days a month. (Think chairman of the board.)

This signifies that your business is so strong that its success is independent of any single team member, including you, the owner. Also, it has clear processes and procedures to run all five areas: sales/marketing, operations, team, finance, and leadership. You have an enterprise-level dashboard that allows you and your team to know the status and health of your business at any given moment. Finally, you have the clear traditions and culture to help keep your business true to its vision, mission, and values even after you aren't present every day.

Since you've built out your systems and developed your management team, you're now ready to take that last step to Level Three.

Level Three:
Owning an Owner-Independent Business

Focus: To determine your desired exit strategy and clarify your personal role in the business

Characteristics of a Typical Level Three Business:

- The business is run by a competent and winning management team independent of the owner (who may still fill one of the roles, but who has a replacement groomed and ready to step in).

- The business runs smoothly whether the owner is there or not over an extended period of time (based on having a solid base of systems, team, controls, and culture).

- Its clients look to the *business*, not the owner, to fulfill promises.

The 3 Exit Strategies for You and Your Level Three Business

Every story needs a great ending or you're left feeling dissatisfied. Your business story needs a great ending, too. We call this your exit strategy.

For Tom, this meant transitioning to own his business passively. He had spent 15 years building his online company, increasing sales, recruiting and nurturing his team, and growing market share. Then on December 10 at 11 A.M. he held an all-hands meeting of his full company to announce his retirement from the business. He shared how much he valued the contributions they had all made, about how their newly promoted CEO would fill Tom's role in the company, and how they would see Tom a few times a month as he kept an eye on how things were going, but that he wanted to spend more time with his family. It was an emotional moment for his company and for Tom, and one that he credits the same insights you've been learning in this book, which he was introduced to six years before when he started working with David's business coaching company to speed up his company's growth.

At that time Tom's business was stuck with sales under $6 million per year and Tom working 80-hour workweeks, fast burning out. Yet here he was six years later and his company had grown sales to just over $20 million per year, Tom had reduced his working hours to under 20 hours a week, and now he was retiring, shifting to own his company passively.

What about you? What's your desired exit strategy for your company? This may or may not mean actually selling your business. In fact, many Level Three business owners choose to stay actively engaged. What's the critical distinction? Continued involvement is a personal choice, not a business *requirement.* That's right. You get to make that decision and choose any of these three main exit strategies:

1. You can sell the business and move on to your next great adventure.
2. You can scale the business to the big time.
3. You can passively own the business, with a greatly diminished role for yourself in its daily operation.

Let's go deeper into each of these three exit strategies so you get a sense of the end toward which you're working.

Exit Strategy 1: Sell

Once you've built a Level Three business, you've created a valuable asset with clear market value. Your first exit strategy is to harvest the equity you've built by selling the business.

Take the case of Jeff Hoffman, David's friend and coauthor of *SCALE.* After college, Jeff started his first software company, CTI, and grew it into a thriving innovator in the travel industry. He strategically positioned the company to be bought out by one of the industry's major players, which is exactly what happened. American Express acquired CTI for more than $10 million.

Since that time, Jeff has gone on to build and later sell other successful companies, including his biggest success to date, cofounding a travel site you may have heard about—Priceline.com.

5 Types of Buyers for Your Level Three Business

When you sell an owner-reliant Middle Stage Level Two business, generally the only interested buyers are mom-and-pop entrepreneurs who want to buy a job for themselves. It's when you reach Advanced Stage Level Two or even an owner-independent Level Three business that you appeal to a wider, more financially capable pool of potential buyers.

These five main types of buyers might be interested in buying your Level Three business:

1. **Strategic buyers:** Strategic buyers look at your business and want to buy it as an operating entity. They want to maximize its value to them after buying it. Usually, this means they want to integrate the business into their existing business frame. This might mean buying your business for assets such as a patent or other technology or trade secrets, for the value of its brand, or for your customer list and relationships.

A strategic buyer could be a competitor, a key customer, or a large vendor, or it could be a new entrant looking to buy into an advantageous position in your industry.

Generally, you'll get the highest price from strategic buyers because they have the opportunity to reduce overhead after the sale by consolidating your business into theirs. They also tend to have the best knowledge and experience to maximize your business afterward, plus they have a high comfort level with your industry, product line, and customer relationships.

2. **Financial buyers:** Financial buyers, most commonly private equity companies, are looking at your business as a financial investment with their eyes squarely on return on investment (ROI). These private equity companies are generally interested in buying only if they can see a clear way to get out of the investment profitably within a three- to five-year time horizon. Remember the case study of Morgan in Chapter 2? This situation involved a sale to a private equity firm. The company that bought Morgan's company did what's called an "industry rollup." This is when an investment group acquires several small to medium-sized companies in a target industry. They intend to integrate these acquisitions into a larger whole that will be worth more because it has acquired a certain scale.

3. **Management buyout (MBO):** This is when the top managers in your company team up to buy you out. Typically, they put up a portion of the purchase price themselves and then find outside investors or financing to cover the remainder of the purchase price. This type of sale tends to be less disruptive to your employees because the management team in place remains essentially the same after the sale.

4. **Employee stock ownership program (ESOP):** This is a special type of sale of the business to its employees. Strong tax incentives support this type, but generally you'd receive the lowest price of all the options if you choose this one.

5. **Going public:** One final way to sell your business is to sell it to the public through a public stock offering. For example, when Jeff Hoffman, whose story we told you about just a moment ago, took Priceline.com public in 1999, the company raised billions of dollars. While going public is primarily a financing strategy to raise capital more than a way to sell the company, after you factor

in the "lockup" period during which insiders can't sell, and the potential adverse impact of putting a large block of stock on the market for sale at any given time, having shares of the company on a public market does allow the owners to sell some or all of their interest in the company.

Steps to Take Today to Sell for Top Dollar Tomorrow

STEPHANIE'S STORY

Jack and I have known for years that one day we would sell our company. Our two kids weren't interested in running it, and we had a large amount of equity that we'd built up over the years as we took the business to Level Three. We knew that selling it would be our way of harvesting that equity.

So several years before we wanted to sell the company we started to plan for the things we could do along the way that would lead to the best valuation and market demand to buy our company down the road.

We did things like normalize our financials, invest in our systems, cultivate and grow our management team, and strategically choose which market and business model to follow. This last item made a huge impact on our valuation. When we first bought the company, it was an injection molding plastics manufacturing company. But when we combined our work with start-ups in Silicon Valley (which was very close to our Santa Cruz, California, facility), helping them rapidly prototype devices, along with our strong operational, production, and quality capabilities, we knew that working to position our company as a medical device manufacturer was the right thing to do. It took us close to five years to make this transition, but when we did, it changed the multiple that buyers were willing to pay for our company by a factor of 10.

The most important question you can ask yourself is this: *"What can I do today to prepare to sell my business two to three years from now?"* Here are three concrete steps to follow as you prepare now to sell later.

Step 1: Determine what your business is currently worth.

How do you find out what your business is currently worth? You can look to industry or association sources for the most common valuation methods for your type of business. You can hire a valuation firm, work with an investment banker, or even hire a CPA experienced in your industry and type of business. Even more important is understanding how companies in your industry and business category are valued by the market. What formula is most commonly used? What is the current range of business multipliers, and how can you command the top end of that range? Find out.

THE 6 KEY RISKS FROM A BUYER'S PERSPECTIVE

1. **Management team:** How talented are the managers? Will they stay? What happens if one or more leave? Who will lead the enterprise as a whole?

2. **Reliance on owner:** Will this business work well without you (the owner) around? Which customers rely on your personal relationship to keep them happy? What banking relationships are based on your personal financials or rapport with a specific banker?

3. **Truth and accuracy of financial records:** Are your financial records clean and up to date? Have your financials been audited by outside firms? Are there any warning flags like discrepancies between corporate tax returns, filings, or investor reporting and the company financials?

4. **Customer base (concentration and future prospects):** Are the customer relationships with the company or with the owner? Is any one customer so big that the business would suffer if that customer's orders diminished or went away altogether? What are the future prospects for your key customers? Your industry? Your specific business?

5. **Competition:** Where does your company stand in the marketplace compared to your competitors? How will you assure your prospective buyer that sales and market share can grow, not just be maintained?

6. **Industry future:** What trends affect your industry? What potential disruptors could kill your industry overnight? What contingencies do you have for these scenarios?

The bottom-line question is this: *"Are you taking action to mitigate as many perceived buyer risks as possible over the next two to three years before you sell?"*

Step 2: Do a "buyer's audit."

Put yourself in the shoes of a potential buyer and take a long, hard look at your business. Which elements give it value in an outsider's eyes? What major risks do you see that scare you? What are the most attractive parts of buying this specific business versus one of its competitors? What are the least attractive parts of buying it? If you could change only three things to make it more attractive as an acquisition, what three specific things would you change over the coming 12 months?

Step 3: Mitigate risks and enhance value.

Once you've identified key risks (see the sidebar, which shows the six key risks) and specific elements that create value, take preemptive action to lessen the buyer's risks and enhance your business's value. The more you mitigate risks and enhance value in the eyes of a future buyer, the more your company will be worth when you sell it.

Mitigating risks is half the equation; the other half is enhancing value. What can you do over the next few years to enhance your business's value? Can you grow your sales? Improve your margins? Develop protected intellectual property? More firmly establish a brand? Deepen competitive advantages? Build company systems? Grow the management team?

5 Mistakes to Avoid

Here are five mistakes that sellers often make when putting their company on the market.

Mistake #1: Stopping before the finish line.

You need to make sure you run your business well *through* its final closing. Many sales fail, and you'd hate to have a sale fall through only to see that your business has trended down, and now your next buyer wants to pay you less. To protect yourself, consider working with the right business broker or investment banker to help run the sales process for you, which will give you the time and emotional distance to run your company well through the closing.

Mistake #2: Deal fatigue.

Selling your company is a marathon, not a sprint. It takes time—don't kid yourself. It may take 12, 24, or even 36 months. Many buyers fall away. Due diligence is a pain. Set your mind that this isn't going to be a 90-day sprint, but rather a longer process that you intend to see through to the end.

Mistake #3: Buyers who are looking for information, not a business.

Sadly, some buyers aren't really buyers—they are simply looking for insider information on your customers, pricing strategy, or key employees. Make sure you also have a solid nondisclosure agreement with strong nonsolicitation provisions. Also, qualify your buyers as to the following:

- Why are they looking to buy your or any business?
- Do they seem viable as a buyer?
- How will they pay?
- What are their business references who can speak to their integrity?
- If the buyer is a publicly traded company, have you researched its Securities and Exchange Commission (SEC) filings?
- Have you spoken with other companies they've acquired? If not, why not?

Mistake #4: Your team *feeling* the rumors.

Be very careful to not let your team find out about a potential sale until you are ready to talk with them. This means speaking with your CFO early and getting him or her to be very careful. Then later, it means bringing your leadership team into the mix, again with clear guidelines to them to be careful about holding this information in confidence. The bottom line is that you must protect your company from the destructive power of the rumor mill.

Mistake #5: Customers finding out too early.

Do not share customer information until late in the sale process. By this time you will know a lot more about your buyer and the buyer's ability and commitment to close. You'll also have clear nonsolicitation and confidentiality provisions in place that your attorney has written up to protect you.

Exit Strategy 2: Scale

We've addressed the concept of scaling throughout the book. In the context of exiting, scaling means that you, the business owner, firmly decide to stay actively involved in the business and grow it magnitudes bigger.

It may seem strange to call scaling an exit strategy, but many entre-preneurs who've built a Level Three business don't want to leave or sell it. Rather, they want to grow it to the next level, which we call scaling your business. This means you take a $15 million company and grow it to $150 million or $1.5 billion. This option gives you the greatest financial reward, but it also requires your continued commitment, often over five or 10 years or even longer after your business has reached Level Three.

For example, Wayne, one of David's clients, partnered with two other founders to build a nuclear medicine testing laboratory chain. Together, they have scaled their company to its current $200 million size. Wayne and his partners still work full-time in the business, driving its growth higher and higher. Building a billion-dollar business is well within their reach. It's an active road for them to follow, and they are choosing the exit strategy of scaling with their eyes wide open.

Exit Strategy 3: Own Passively

Once you've taken your business to Level Three, you can transition to a more passive role—owning the company without running it every day. Think back to Tom's story of announcing his retirement and of his replacement in his online business with a key team member being pro-moted to CEO. Stephanie owned her manufacturing company for sev-eral years as a Level Three business, enjoying a seven-figure income and working only part-time. David has owned several Level Three companies that he kept a close eye on, but that required very little of his day-to-day involvement.

If you choose this exit strategy, you'll enjoy the ongoing cash flow from the business without regularly coming into the office. You'll still have responsibilities, but from an *owner's* viewpoint, not a CEO's or a manager's viewpoint.

10 Tips to Successfully Step into the Chairman's Role Versus the CEO's More Active Role

1. Remember that you must work through your CEO and help empower him or her.

2. You are a sounding board where your CEO can go to for feed-back, support, and fresh ideas.

3. You must set clear expectations with your CEO. What informa-tion do you want the CEO to share? When? How often? What deliverables is the CEO responsible for? How will you hold him or her accountable? How do you want to be kept in the loop on progress and challenges?

4. Be careful about unintentionally undercutting your CEO by being too active in the business. This is especially true when your team is used to seeing you lead the day-to-day business. Refer them back to the CEO for answers. Share your feedback through your CEO. When you visit, you are there to connect, encourage, and learn. Be careful about directing things like you used to when you are physically on-site.

5. Make sure your management team has a written business plan with clearly defined goals and strategies that you are in full agreement with. Then hold them accountable for delivering these results. In other words, set them up to win by making the rules, boundaries, and goals of the game very clear. Update this plan annually.

6. Make sure the business has a solid "scoreboard" that lays out its key enterprise metrics. Review this scoreboard weekly or monthly. If you see something troubling or puzzling, address it right away through the CEO.

7. Each month review the financials and key department scoreboards. Then meet with your CEO for status updates on key initiatives and other information.

8. Make sure all compensation is in alignment with your strategy and company mission, vision, and values.

A SHORT QUIZ TO DETERMINE WHERE YOU ARE ON THE LEVEL THREE MAP

Now that we've gone through the complete life cycle of your business from Level One to Level Three, what level and stage is your business in right now? Circle the statement that at present best describes your business:

Level One: You're still working on your business plan, raising your startup funding, and preparing to launch your new business.

Early Stage Level Two: Your business is in its infancy, scrambling to make those early sales and fulfill customer promises.

Middle Stage Level Two: Your business is sustainable. It works, but only if you're present to work for it. You're the main producer and director around whom your company revolves.

Advanced Stage Level Two: Your business is growing fast, with leaders in two or more of your five core pillars. You're in the process of refining your business systems and building your management team.

Level Three: Your business is firing on all cylinders, with leaders in at least four of your five core pillars. Your business is systems reliant and ready for you to choose your exit strategy—to sell, scale, or own passively.

---

9. Beware your urge to step back in. You can undercut your CEO if you are not careful.

10. Beware your counter-urge to just ignore the business; it's probably your greatest asset, so pay attention on a weekly and monthly basis and "manage by exceptions."

Most Level Three business owners we know (including ourselves) spend between five and 25 hours a month managing their business interests when things run smoothly. In the event they aren't performing well, taking a more active role may be necessary.

A Little-Known Formula at the Heart of 325 of the Forbes 400

Before leaving this chapter, let's talk about how taking your business to Level Three impacts the *value* of your business. We've hinted at this earlier, but now we want to address it head-on.

Have you ever wondered how the wealthiest people in the world originally built their fortunes? If you analyzed the Forbes 400 list of the richest people in the United States, you'd find that more than 325 of them got on the list by applying a simple formula (or being the heir of someone who applied this formula!). What is this formula? It's called a "business multiplier," and it's one of the greatest wealth leverage points of all time.

Let's explore the business multiplier concept by walking through the value of a fictitious business we'll call Maui, Inc. as it progresses through the Level Three Map.

Level One: Business Start-Up
Value: Zero

You probably already know that a business start-up is nothing more than an idea and a plan; as such, it has no value in the market. The only exception to this might be if the plan has intellectual property attached to it such as a patent that will be applied or a trade secret process that will be leveraged. So at Level One, the business value of our imaginary business, Maui, Inc., is *zero*.

Early Stage Level Two: Business Scrambling for Its Survival
Value: Very Little

At Early Stage Level Two, this business has few paying customers. It's desperately trying to secure more clients and fulfill its promises to them long enough to establish a secure base for the business.

At this stage, Maui, Inc. still has no real value other than that of its tangible assets, including its equipment, inventory, and fixtures (and even those won't be valued at more than a fraction of original cost), or some deeply discounted value of its current annual sales.

Middle Stage Level Two: A Successful Business That Revolves around the Owner

Gross Sales:	**$500,000**
Operating Profit:	**$150,000**
Value:	**$150,000**

Once Maui, Inc. has a consistent track record of generating profits, it gains value. But that value will be limited because the business depends on the owner being present and involved.

While every business has a different valuation formula, most owner-reliant Middle Stage Level Two businesses end up valued in the $50,000 to $500,000 range. The actual value will depend on the industry, the length of operating history, the value of its hard assets (e.g., inventory, equipment, etc.), and the sales volume of the business. But the biggest limitation to selling a Middle Stage Level Two business is its limited pool of buyers. Usually only mom-and-pop buyers will step into the owner's shoes and "own" their own jobs. Plus they have very little access to any large capital sources, which limits what they can afford to pay.

With Maui, Inc., let's make these two assumptions: (1) It's a service business with a profit margin of 30 percent, meaning 30 cents out of every dollar of sales ends up as operating profit. (2) Its gross sales are $500,000, which means the business nets $150,000 per year.

So in this hypothetical example, we're pegging the value of Maui, Inc. at $150,000, which is one times (1×) its annual operating income.

Advanced Stage Level Two: A Successful Business Much Less Reliant on the Owner's Presence to Function

Gross Sales:	**$3.4 million**
Operating Profit:	**$1 million**
Value:	**$3 million**

Once Maui, Inc. hits Advanced Stage Level Two, it has key leaders employed in three of its core pillars. The business still benefits from the owner's leadership, but the company is becoming more systems reliant every day. Sales are climbing fast. In fact, gross sales are $3.4 million and operating profit is $1 million per year.

While that $1 million profit sure feels good, even better is being an Advanced Stage Level Two business. At this stage, Maui, Inc. is now valued by a special formula called a business multiplier. The company is now valued at a multiple of its operating profit, which is a simplification but an accurate one. Every industry has its own range of business multipliers used in valuing a business in that industry.

Here's the best part. As you progress to Level Three, not only is your business more valuable because you're increasing both gross sales and operating profits, but you're also increasing the business multiplier that your business can command. For example, your business at Advanced Stage Level Two might command only a three or four times (3–4X) multiplier, but when you hit Level Three, you might command an eight or 10 times (8–10X) multiplier.

In our example, at Advanced Stage Level Two we value Maui, Inc. at three times (3X) its operating profit, or $3 million. Let's see what happens when Maui, Inc. reaches Level Three.

Level Three: A Systems-Reliant Business with Winning Management Team in Place

Gross Sales:	**$10 million**
Operating Profit:	**$3 million**
Value:	**$21 million**

By this point, your Level Three business operates like a well-oiled machine. Your winning management team is in place, and your business controls and systems allow you to scale the business.

In our example, Maui, Inc. has grown its gross sales to $10 million, providing $3 million per year of operating profit. As a Level Three business, Maui, Inc. now commands a seven times (7X) business multiplier, pegging its value at seven times (7X) its operating profit, or $21 million!

Notice that sales at Maui, Inc. have grown by only 300 percent from when the business was an Advanced Stage Level Two business, but it's now worth seven times more. This demonstrates the multiplying power of leveraging a higher business multiplier!

Here's an example of how this all works in the real world. Let's return to Jennifer, the winner of our national business search contest we told you about earlier. When we started working together, her company was an owner-reliant Middle Stage Level Two business with annual sales of $1.2 million. Twelve months later, she had not only increased her sales to $2 million, but in the process, she had grown her business to Advanced Stage Level Two. Let's look at how this maturation of her business radically increased its value.

As a Middle Stage Level Two business, the pool of potential buyers for Jennifer's company was much smaller. That means fewer people want and can afford to pay for the business. Assuming she could get two times (2X) operating profit for her business at that stage (a realistic amount for this type of business at Middle Stage Level Two), this increased the value of her business from $750,000 to $1.5 million.

But she didn't only increase sales and profits. Jennifer took her business to Advanced Stage Level Two, reduced its reliance on her, created more durable systems, and began to scale her company. This likely doubled her business multiplier from two times (2X) her operating profit to four times (4X). This meant that 12 months after she won the contest, her company was worth $3 million. Think about it. Her $800,000 increase in sales along with maturing the business to Advanced Stage Level Two added *$2 million of enterprise equity!* How else could you earn $2 million in 12 months starting with an asset like hers?

But Jennifer's story doesn't end there. Since that time she has grown her sales by several million dollars per year more. And she has taken it very close to, if not reached, Level Three. Today her company is likely worth $18 million to $20 million, which is **1,000 percent more** than it was worth just seven years earlier.

In the next chapter, we go deeper into the five core pillars that will support your Level Three business.

CHAPTER 4

The 5 Functional Pillars of Every Business

Every business has five functional areas that carry the load and provide a stable base to support additional growth; that's why we call them pillars. The five pillars are:

1. **Sales and Marketing**—Responsible for defining your market, finding prospective customers, and generating sales.

2. **Operations**—Fulfills the promises the sales department makes, plus handles back-office functions.

3. **Human Resources, or Team**—Responsible for hiring, training, and reviewing your staff. It also makes sure you comply with local, state, and federal labor laws.

4. **Finance**—Deals with the accounting, manages your cash flow, and pays your bills.

5. **Leadership**—Responsible for the big-picture vision and strategy of your business. Leadership sets the direction, establishes priorities, and coordinates all efforts and resources affecting the other four pillars.

Let's look at each of these five pillars in detail. Remember, while your business may not have formally separated its activities into these divisions, it absolutely carries out each of these five functions, because every business must. So as you read this section, look for ways you can apply various concepts, strategies, and tactics to upgrade your base and handle additional growth so you can expand and scale your business.

Pillar 1: Sales and Marketing

No leads, no sales. No sales, no business. It's that simple.

Marketing is everything you do to get one of your offers in front of the right prospective buyers under the best conditions possible. Marketing crafts your company's identity and positions it in the hearts and minds of your marketplace so you consistently generate the volume of sales leads you need. You want leads that are primed and ready for your selling systems to convert into thrilled clients or repurchasers.

Sales is everything you do to make your offers as effective as possible and to close selling opportunities. Your offers can be delivered in a variety of ways—from trained sales reps to a call center taking phone calls to a sales letter or print ad to an interactive website to a trade show team to a retail location. Remember, the Sales and Marketing Pillar finds clients, makes sales, and generates revenue; it's the part of your business that makes it rain cash.

Too many entrepreneurs only focus on this pillar because they *have* to, not because they *want* to. They feel intimidated by the idea of selling. But understand this: **In Early and Middle Stage Level Two, it's crucial for you as the company founder to focus a majority of your energy on generating profitable sales.** If you don't, your new business won't survive, let alone thrive. Only as you grow your business can you replace yourself from the functions of this pillar. Achieving that requires creating a profitable selling *system.*

In the early days of your business, you focus on making sure sales happen, which means meeting with clients and closing deals yourself. Later, however, you must shift your focus to creating repeatable and scalable selling systems that don't depend on your involvement.

For example, imagine you have a new software start-up. As the company founder, your early efforts will involve landing key joint venture relationships with established players in your industry so you can market through their existing client base and split the revenue generated. As your software company grows, you no longer meet personally with new joint venture partners. Instead, you focus on finding and hiring the talent to do that. Later, you'll ensure your business is developing systems that will consistently find and hire new sales talent for your team.

Or imagine you have a contracting business. Early on, you meet with prospective clients to give estimates and close sales. But this is a Level Two solution. To create a Level Three business, you need to build the *system* that generates those sales. This might mean creating advertising systems to generate leads, hiring and training new estimators to close business, and eventually hiring a sales and marketing manager to take over this pillar of your contracting business.

Plus, without these sales and marketing systems, too many companies fall prey to "feast or famine" cycles that make it stressful and difficult to plan staffing, production, and other investments.

Your systems in this pillar of your company include:

- **Lead generation** systems to consistently generate the lead volume needed to generate sales.

- **Lead conversion** systems to consistently convert leads into thrilled clients.

- **Tracking and reporting** systems to reliably measure the effectiveness of your marketing and sales efforts, allowing you to optimize your selling systems over time.

Because many sales systems employ live sales agents to close sales, your system might also need to include the processes you use to find, hire, and train new sales agents. Add to that the sales management processes you develop to lead, motivate, and grow your sales team over time. None of this is easy, but the rewards are huge.

DAVID'S STORY

One of the companies I built originally was dependent on my partner and me to produce all the sales—and sell we did. The two of us generated several million dollars of sales each year. But it required long hours and, even worse (from my perspective), lots of travel. In those days, I had to spend 10 days out of every month on the road selling and closing new business. Although I was making a lot of money, this sure wasn't the dream I had for myself.

Then we finally got smart and began building a sales team and systems that didn't need us to close sales. We built up our online sales to half a million dollars a year. We built a network of independent sales reps who sold another two to three million dollars' worth a year. And we created a whole new selling channel with joint venture partners that generated several million dollars of annual sales (split 50–50 with our joint venture partner).

All told, it took us 36 months to build and optimize these selling systems. In the process, we tripled our company's sales volume while radically reducing the dependence on my partner and me to generate sales. Best of all, I cut my travel time by 70 percent!

---

8 Sales and Marketing Questions Every Business Owner Must Ask

1. **What are your most effective systems for generating new leads for your business?** For example, referral relationships, digital advertising, affiliate program, social media, display advertisements in industry journals, and trade shows.

2. **How could you scale up the best of these systems to bring in more business?** For example, establish clear tracking to ensure you know which leads are the right leads, scale up your ad buys or send out more marketing pieces, optimize your website for better search engine results, spend more on winning key word advertising campaigns, and create formalized referral programs.

3. **How can you make these lead generation systems more consistent, reliable, or dependable?** For example, create a master marketing calendar with clear dates and assigned deliverables, establish a proven control ad or direct mail letter, have a sales web- site used by your prospective customers who come to shop or gather information, and establish clear metrics that allow you to know objectively what is and isn't working.

4. **What are your least effective lead generation systems?** This is the best place to look when searching for ways to grow your business. Too many business owners try to fix or improve their bottom 30 to 50 percent. They'd be better off cutting these losing efforts and immediately reinvesting the saved time and money into scaling the top 20 percent of their lead generators.

5. **What are your most effective systems for closing sales?** For example, live salespeople, direct mail letters, long-form sales landing web pages, and sales video online.

6. **How could you scale up the best of these systems or better use them with the leads you already have?** For example, hire more sales reps, invest in technology to better handle the lead flow you currently have, create an automated follow-up selling system, design a website to effectively sell, and move from selling one-to-one to one-to-many by hosting online webinars or live events.

7. **How can you make these sales conversion systems more consistent, reliable, or dependable?** For example, draft a best sales script, create a PowerPoint template for your entire sales team to use to make their sales presentations, and so on.

8. **What are your least effective sales conversion systems?** Again, this is the place to make immediate improvements to your sales in the shortest period of time. Rather than fix them, scrap your losing systems and leverage the selling systems that are working best. At the very least, take the elements of your winning sales systems (e.g., scripting, offer, pricing, sales logic, etc.) and incorporate them in your worst performers.

Scale Your Winners and Starve Your Losers

With the possible exception of your Finance Pillar, in no other area of your business is it as important to track your results as in sales and marketing. Do that by creating simple scorecards that tell you what *is* and *is not* working.

Do you know quantitatively and objectively how each of your main lead generation activities performs? For example, do you know your cost per lead by lead source? Do you know your percentage response rates (e.g., click-through rates on banner ads, or response rates per direct mail piece, etc.)? Are you able to relate your lead generation activities to your sales conversion metrics so you can track which leads are highest (or lowest) quality?

After you have good numerical data with which to work, determine your best lead generators, your best lead converters, and your best current client resellers, and invest in scaling up those efforts. How do you get the resources to do this? Easy. Starve your losers. Cut your bottom performers. Don't waste precious time, focus, and money on below-average performers when you can reinvest these resources in scaling up the best ones. We also encourage you to access the Business Owner Tool Kit we created to complement this book. In it, the *"Grow Your Sales Short Course"* gives you five powerful sales and marketing videos to systematically increase your revenues. You can access this free resource at **www.MauiMastermind.com/freetoolkit**. (See Appendix A for full details.)

Pillar 2: Operations

Your Operations Pillar is the part of your business that creates the products or delivers the services your business offers, fulfills promises made by the Sales and Marketing Pillar, and performs the general and administrative back-end functions of your business.

No company will thrive without having a well-organized, strong Operations Pillar. Sure, you can generate sales, but unless you're able to fulfill the promises you've made, your business won't last.

Building Your Master System

Of the many steps to effectively build your Operations Pillar, the first is to build a draft of your master system—your system of how you will store, organize, access, and update *all* your systems. We call this master system your UBS.

DAVID'S STORY

Twenty years ago when I was hard at work building my first successful business, my partner and I came up with the idea of creating a company that would be independent of both of us. Although I hadn't developed the language and finer distinctions of a Level Three business, in essence, that's what we were attempting to build.

We laid out our dream on an oversized sheet of white poster paper (which I still have in my archive), calling it our "Business System." When we abbreviated that two-word phrase, we ran into a little trouble, so we quickly added the word "Ultimate." Now we had the acronym UBS.

Our Ultimate Business System (UBS) was the collection of processes, procedures, checklists, and other systems we spent the next five years refining. In fact, in our company, UBS became both a noun and a verb. We'd say things like, *"Great idea to lower costs, Paige. Can you please add that to the USB so that other team members can use it?"* It was a verb when we used it to say things like, *"Beth, can you please UBS that process so we don't have the same problems next time?"*

UBS'ing became a discipline and an obsession in our business, and it's one I strongly urge you to adopt for your company. It's a philosophy of capturing winning processes and best practices into repeatable, scalable systems. It's also a clear structure within which to organize and house your growing collection of business systems.

---

4 Steps to Build Your UBS

Your UBS is the master system for how your company structures, organizes, stores, accesses, refines, and, if need be, deletes its systems.

More important, your UBS is the doorway through which you can move your team to start making systems a *daily* conversation and discipline inside your company.

Now, to be clear here, we are *not* talking about a policies and procedures manual. After surveying thousands of businesspeople about the usefulness of a policies and procedures manual, we've come to one firm and irrefutable conclusion—no one uses or refers to a policies and procedures manual, especially after the first 30 days on the job (and most won't really use it even during that time either!)

Think of your UBS as an organized collection of tools that captures the actual, everyday know-how of your business in a searchable, accessible, and editable way. These tools are held inside a simple structure of file folders, generally on a cloud-based system, and include things like your checklists, spreadsheets, proposal templates, training videos, and sample marketing pieces.

Without a UBS, likely you'll have a hodgepodge collection of files spread on a dozen different team members' computers or, even worse, locked informally in their heads. When John creates a better version of a process, without a formal UBS these improvements likely just stay with John. When Sarah figures out how to do a key function, she may write a few notes for herself on yellow stickies posted on the side of her desk. If she were ever to leave the company, all those notes would get swept into the trash can and all that valuable company knowledge would be lost.

Your UBS is a way to start gathering into one place your systems, making sure that your whole team has access to best practices and key institutional knowledge that previously was locked in the heads of a few key people.

The UBS concept also is the best way to start the dialogue of systems inside your company. Your ultimate goal is to make your UBS a living, breathing way of doing business in your company—an ongoing practice.

You'll know you've won when you regularly hear your team say things like, *"Did you add that to the UBS?"* and *"Great solution to that problem—can you UBS it?"*

Here is the simple four-step process to start building your UBS in the next 90 days.

Step One: Create your UBS's file folder organizational hierarchy.

If you had to cluster all the functions of your business into five to nine main folders/areas, what would they be? (See Figure 4.1.)

1.0 Sales/Marketing

1.1 Lead Generation

1.2 Lead Conversion

1.3 Planning and Strategy

1.4 Branding

2.0 Operations

2.1 General Administration

2.2 Production

2.3 Fulfillment

2.4 Customer Service

2.5 Purchasing

5.0 Leadership

5.1 Strategic Planning

5.2 Leadership Dev/Continuity

5.3 Company Culture

5.4 Communication
   Companywide

4.0 Team

4.1 Hiring/Onboarding

4.2 Training/Review/Retention

4.3 Compliance

4.4 Outsourcing

4.5 Exit Processes

3.0 Financial

3.1 Accounting/Reporting

3.2 A/R (Collections)

3.3 A/P (Payables)

3.4 Budgeting and Planning

3.5 Financial Controls

3.6 Cash Flow Management

Your "UBS" is your "Ultimate Business System". It is your master system for how you organize, store, access, and refine your systems. Your goal is to make your UBS a living, breathing way of doing business in your company. You'll know you've won when you regularly hear your team say things like, *"Did you add that to the UBS?"* and *"Great solution to that problem, can you UBS it?"* This is not something you'll do in one sitting, but rather it is a way of approaching your business that you'll engage your entire team in owning over the long term.

Figure 4.1: Your Master System
Copyright © Maui Mastermind®

If you ran a medical practice, your UBS folders might look like this:

1.0 Marketing

2.0 HR

3.0 Clinical

4.0 Administrative/Operations

5.0 Financial

6.0 Leadership

If you owned a manufacturing company, your UBS folders might include:

1.0 Business Development

2.0 Production and Purchasing

3.0 Quality

4.0 Engineering

5.0 Administration

6.0 HR

7.0 Leadership

Step Two: Pick *one* area to start with, and break that one area down into five to seven subareas.

For example, if you ran a medical group and chose "2.0 HR," to start with your subareas might look like this:

2.0 HR

2.1 Recruitment and Hiring

2.2 Onboarding and Orientation

2.3 Training

2.4 Benefits and HR Admin

2.5 Exiting

The key is to start with *one* area of your UBS and build from there.

Step Three: Populate this one area, and its five to seven subareas, with any of your existing systems.

Look through each of your team's hard drives and see what systems you already have. You'll be surprised at how many of these systems will be known to only one person. And you'll be horrified to notice how many out-of-date versions of some of your key systems people are still using because they don't know there is an updated version to it.

You might have a scheduling spreadsheet you use to organize which staff members are on which shifts month by month, a nine-step checklist to open up your store for the day, and even a database of potential suppliers to get bids from on new product orders.

As you go through your team's computers and files to gather existing systems and tools and put them into your new UBS, this is a perfect time to identify which tools are outdated or inadequate, which work well, and which tools your system desperately needs.

Save to your UBS only those documents and tools that you want your business to actually use going forward. (You can always store anything no longer current in an "archive" folder in each section of your UBS on the off chance you need to access it later.)

KEY POINT: Rename all files you put into your UBS so that they are obvious and easy to search for later. Think Google and key words here. Don't name a file based on what the person who created it thinks it should be; name it in terms of what a new user of that file will *search* for it under. Standardize your key naming conventions (or start to, at any rate) at this point. Are you going to call this type of report a "scoreboard" or "dashboard" or some other term?

The lesson here is that team members will look for a tool by searching a folder in your UBS. If they don't quickly and easily find what they want, they'll give up and either just re-create the tool or wing it. By naming your files to make them intuitive and easy to find, not only will the team use the right tool, but your systems will get the benefit of any refinement your team members make as they actually use your systems in the performance of their day-to-day jobs.

Step Four: Pick one or two systems to build this quarter for this area of the business.

Ask yourself, *"If we could only build one or two systems in this area of the business in the next 90 days, which one or two systems would be most valuable to create first?"*

Notice that as you involve your team in doing these four simple steps, you have a chance to talk with them about the value of systems, and how they benefit each team member and the company as a whole. Share with them your and your company's commitment to being a systems-driven culture, and ask for their help in taking the first key steps to get started on this process.

Then each quarter, repeat steps two to four.

Over time, this process is magic and you'll find that you consistently make your business more and more scalable and less and less reliant on a few key staff members (including you).

Systems and controls cannot be a fad, but must be an ingrained way of doing things inside your business. If you start the process and don't see it through, your efforts will wither and you'll lose credibility with your team. Your team must see why systems and controls matter to the business, to you, and to them. And they must see you staying the course with making those systems and controls a fundamental part of your business.

To watch a video training on creating and harnessing your UBS, see the "Scaling Operations Short Course" that we've included with the Business Owner Tool Kit. You can access this free resource at **www.MauiMastermind.com/freetoolkit**. (See Appendix A for full details.)

Where to Store Your UBS

Every company needs to come up with its own way of storing its systems for its team to use. Technologies change. But at its bottom, your UBS requires storage with the following four attributes:

1. **Accessible:** It needs to be accessible—fast. Usually, this means it's a cloud-based instead of a paper-based system, too.

2. **Searchable:** It needs to be easily searchable. People have to be able to quickly find what they want or they'll start to keep their own "cheat sheet" systems at their desks or on their computers. This would eventually mean your UBS won't house the best practices but be merely a historical procedural manual that no one really uses.

3. **Version control:** It needs to be collaborative, which means all users need to be able to edit and improve the data. This requires having version control and also means being constantly pruned of outdated information and systems. Systems will change and grow, and if you leave the old ones to live with the new, they will cloud the waters and make it harder for people to know quickly

which systems to use and when. In many ways, the *eraser* is mightier than the *pen* for your UBS.

4. **Security:** It needs to have secure features that allow you to protect your intellectual property both from outside parties and from internal misuse. Regard your UBS as one of your business's most valuable assets.

What matters most is that you map out the architecture of how your UBS will be organized. That way, no matter which software or hardware you use to store it, you'll have a good start on an organized, useful way to create, store, access, and refine all your business systems.

Pillar 3: Team

Your Team Pillar establishes how you hire, orient, train, assess, compensate, and, if necessary, let go of your staff. It deals with your policies and procedures for team members and the legal requirements of working with employees.

To grow most businesses, you'll need talented team members to both spark and support that growth. Whether it's adding sales team members to increase sales or engineers to design products or accounting staff to keep track of the money, your company's greatest source of leverage is your company's ability to attract, hire, integrate, and empower talented, committed people to play on your team.

Too many businesses never tap into even a fraction of the true talents of their team members. What a catastrophic loss—one that their owners may never even understand. But not your business. Make sure you engage your team in helping build your systems and design scalable solutions.

Here are some of the key systems you'll need to build for your Team Pillar to function optimally:

- Hiring processes
- New team member orientation process
- Regular staff evaluation process
- Team training
- Compliance procedures for all applicable labor laws
- Troubleshooting and personality challenges
- Exit process both for friendly partings and expedited exits (e.g., firings)

Pillar 4: Finance

The Finance Pillar of your business encompasses all the essential functions of collecting, tracking, distributing, and reporting the flow of money in and out of your business. It includes your billing procedures, collection practices, and accounts payable processes. It also includes all financial reporting from balance sheets to profit and loss statements to statements of cash flow. All of these help your management team make better business decisions.

At Level One and Early Stage Level Two, chances are you have few financial systems in place. *This is normal for a small business scrambling to survive.* At the very least, we suggest outsourcing your bookkeeping to a part-time service so your financial transactions are accurately entered into an accounting software. It's okay at this stage in your business to live with messiness; your main focus must be on establishing sales and developing your core operational processes. Just make sure this doesn't become habitual.

Entering Middle Stage Level Two requires putting your financial house in order. Whether you outsource your accounting to a part-time controller or hire on someone full-time, it's essential that you enlist help to organize the financial area and begin establishing intelligent financial controls that your business will need as it grows.

At Advanced Stage Level Two, you'll most likely have a full-time controller overseeing the Finance Pillar of your business, perhaps even with one or two data entry helpers.

As you enter Level Three, you'll probably have a full-blown chief financial officer (CFO) working for your business, not just a controller. What's the difference? A controller is expert in following the financial systems you have in place; a CFO is expert in helping you build them. A controller can help you make sure you have accurate reporting and can maintain your existing financial infrastructure; a CFO can help you with higher-order financial thinking, such as running pro forma analyses and managing your credit lines. A controller can help you execute plans in the here and now; a CFO will help you plan for the future. And as your business grows, you'll need the high-order expertise of a competent CFO.

Pillar 5: Executive Leadership

The final pillar of your business is Executive Leadership—the area that leads your leaders and sets the big-picture direction for your company.

It's also likely the final area for you to personally let go of. Remember, many Level Three business owners *choose* to stay in their businesses as CEOs and to continue working. The key distinction is that this is a *choice*; it's not a requirement for their companies' survival. Successful business owners groom their successors and ready their organizations to successfully transition leadership when they feel the time is right.

As the leader of your business, you have these four main responsibilities:

1. **Setting the big-picture vision for the business.** This means clarifying your vision, mission, and values so they become tangible and meaningful in the lives of your stakeholders. It also means establishing the direction and long-term objectives of your organization.

2. **Defining the big-picture strategy to reach your business goals.** What is your plan of action? How will you allocate your top resources of time, attention, talent, and money to help your company reach its most important goals?

3. **Growing, grooming, and integrating your leadership team.** This means building and leading your leadership team, and creating the strategic structure under which it operates.

4. **Dreaming up what comes next.** As the leader, you must keep looking toward tomorrow to make sure your business stays vibrant and relevant as the world—and your clients' needs—change. Complacency in a changing world is fatal.

On a macro level, your job as leader is establishing what your business stands for and how it sees itself—that is, where it's focused and toward what end it's moving.

Leaders create the narrative through which all stakeholders interpret the business and their relationship to it. *Meaning drives emotion; emotion drives behavior.* As you grow your business, it becomes increasingly important that you shape the stories and traditions that will become part of your company's heritage. These hold your business on course even when you're no longer present each day to drive it.

On a micro level, you want to create a business in which all team members understand their roles, know what they're responsible for, how success in their role will be measured, and how leaders and team members will provide feedback as they go.

What Business Do You Want to Build?

Too many business owners get so caught up in the day-to-day running of their companies that they never step back and think through—on paper—precisely what kind of business they want. One of your key responsibilities as the leader of your business is to create a clear, concrete, and inspirational picture of the business you and your team are working to build.

What business do you want to build over the next three to five years? What does it look like? What's its gross revenue? Operating profit? Key margins? How many customers does it serve? What are the trends in these areas?

What about the qualitative picture of your business? Who are your team members and what are their qualities and roles? How do you measure the success of your business in the lives of your clients?

What do you anticipate your eventual exit strategy will be? What elements will you need to have in place to execute that exit strategy to greatest effect?

Taking time to clarify and describe the business you're working to build *up front* will save you mountains of time, energy, and frustration.

The Level Three Business Audit™

To get where you want to go, you first have to know your starting point. We've developed a proprietary assessment tool to help you determine your business's exact starting point. It's called the *Level Three Business Audit.*

This 128-question tool not only helps you strategically dissect your business and identify its strengths, weaknesses, and key leverage points, but it also places your business in its exact location on the Level Three Map. We use it as the first step we take with any business coaching client we accept into our program.

Let's go through an *abridged* version of this assessment so you can clearly see where your business currently stands. As you rate your business on these 30 areas (six for each pillar of your business), notice what your answers reveal about its position on the Level Three Map.

Total your scores for each pillar and for your business as a whole. Don't worry; it isn't important that you score high now, because what matters is not *where you start* but *where you end up.* And to end up where you want to be, it's critical to have a reliable way of evaluating current positions along the way. This abridged Level Three Business Audit is a simple tool to help you do just that.

SCORE YOUR BUSINESS PILLARS

Rate your business pillars in each of the six areas listed on a scale from 1 to 10 (with 1 being lowest and 10 being highest). For example, under "lead generation," if you think your business does a fantastic job at consistently generating new leads, give yourself a 9 or 10. If your business struggles to find new leads, barely generating enough to keep it afloat, give yourself a 2 or 3. Total your score for each pillar (possible high score of 60 for each pillar), and then total your score for the entire audit. When you're done with this mini audit, we'll explain how to use the results.

Sales and Marketing Pillar:

Lead generation   _____

Lead conversion   _____

Client repeat business   _____

Client upgrade business   _____

Revenue growth (current)   _____

Future prospects for revenue growth   _____

Total

Operations Pillar:

General administrative function   _____

Performance of client work or fulfillment of
client orders   _____

Clients' rating of your company's performance   _____

Cost controls for operation of your business   _____

Business infrastructure (website, physical location,
equipment, etc.)   _____

Scalability of your core product or service   _____

Total   _____

Team Pillar:

Communication systems for team to work together   _____

Having the right team in the right positions   _____

Systems for bringing on new team members   _____

Systems for training and reviewing team members   _____

All team members have a clear understanding of: _____

- What their jobs are.
- How they are expected to perform them.
- How their work will be measured.
- How their work contributes to the bigger picture of the company's mission.
- How their work adds value to the lives of your clients.

Strategy and use of outsourced solutions   _____

Total   ══════════

Finance Pillar:

Accurate and timely financial reporting   _____

Budgeting   _____

Financial controls   _____

Collection systems for accounts receivable   _____

Effective management and use of financing   _____

Cash flow management in general   _____

Total   ══════════

Executive Leadership Pillar:

Each team member has a clear understanding of: _____

- The vision, mission, and values of the company.
- The company's big-picture goals, strategy, and priorities.

Current business strategy   _____

Review process for company performance, direction, strategy, and development   _____

Troubleshooting major challenges when they come up   _____

Leadership training   _____

Company culture and tradition   _____

Total   ══════════

Complete score for your business (scale of 30–300):   _____

If you have an **Early** or **Middle Stage Level Two** business, chances are your scores are currently quite low in three or more pillars. This is normal. You'll improve them rapidly when you follow the Level Three Map and mature your business. The two most important pillars at these stages are your Sales/Marketing Pillar and your Operations Pillar. If either scored below a 20 (out of a possible 60 for the area), then you have concentrated work ahead to improve these two critical pillars. At this time in your business, if you score low in reliably generating leads, closing on sales, or fulfilling your promises, you need to immediately remedy that situation. *These functions are the minimum requirements to have a sustainable business.* Remember, basic survival is the first hurdle to get to Level Three.

If you own an **Advanced Stage Level Two** or **Level Three** business, chances are your scores in most pillars are high (above 40 for each pillar). Look for any specific pillar in which your score was below 20. It needs immediate attention.

You're encouraged to repeat this assessment twice a year. Make sure to date and save your scores so you can track your progress over time. This will give you a simple, structured way to score your business, know where it's progressing, and determine where it needs more of your attention.

CHAPTER 5

6 Time Mastery Strategies to Claim Back Up to a Full Day Each Week to Build Your Business

---

Congratulations on making it this far in the book. By now, you have a real sense for the map you'll follow to build an owner-independent company, and why if you don't, you'll get caught in the Self-Employment Trap.

In this chapter you'll learn a powerful time mastery system to reclaim your best time—eight hours or more each week—to reinvest in upgraded, higher-value uses to grow your company. We're not going to ask you to work longer or harder; that's the problem, not the solution. As you've learned in this book, growing your company simply by putting in more hours is illusory. Yes, like sugar, putting in more hours gives you a short- term burst of production, but the cost to your company's health and the adverse impacts on your life are too great. Plus, there are only so many hours in the day, and at some point growth based purely on you digging in and working longer hours will max out.

Instead, these time mastery strategies will help you fundamentally change the way you see your working time, and use structure to consistently give yourself weekly and daily *blocks* of time with which to do your highest-value work.

We can already anticipate that some readers will say, *"But, David and Stephanie, I'm so busy doing the job of my business that I don't have time to step back and build my business as a business."* That makes about as much sense as running full speed on an exercise treadmill and thinking that if you run faster, you'll make it off the treadmill. The solution isn't to work harder; it's to get off the treadmill by working *smarter*.

Let's get real here. There's no such thing as having more time. We all have all the time there is. While we can change where we *invest* our time, we can't make more of it. The most successful entrepreneurs have learned to invest their time for the best and highest return for their businesses.

In this chapter, we offer six powerful time mastery strategies to upgrade the time you previously spent doing low-value activities to build the business you really want.

You don't have to work nights and weekends to build your Level Three business. Working longer hours is never the answer. Making better choices with how you structure your use of time is the best way to gain more time—both to build your business and just for pleasure.

Pop Quiz: 10 Hours of Time Guaranteed

Would you like to participate in a simple exercise to gain an extra 10 hours or more each week without any extra effort or strain? Then we invite you to play along and answer the following questions:

How many hours do you spend *per week* on average doing the following activities?

_____hours	Watching TV or streaming movies
_____hours	Social media or randomly surfing the web
_____hours	Doing low-value emails
_____hours	Doing office work you could pay someone $50/hour or less to do (filing, faxing, copying, typing, shipping, cleaning, etc.)
_____hours	Doing personal activities you could pay someone $50/hour or less to do (laundry, cleaning, yard work, simple repair work, personal errands, etc.)
TOTAL:	_____hours per week

If you're like most who take this pop quiz, you've probably found well over 10 hours a week that you could redirect into building your business if you made different choices. But heck, that was too easy, so we'll use that as a warm-up to the subject of your personal use of time.

As a business owner, you know that time is one of the most powerful variables you control in the success equation.

Many years ago, famed college basketball coach John Wooden said, *"It's what you learn after you think you know it all that really matters."* You'll get the most out of these tips on time mastery if you keep Coach Wooden's timeless advice in mind and approach this section of the book fresh.

Let's start by clearly stating we understand that, like every other business owner we've ever coached, you probably don't feel you have the time to do what we suggest. In fact, when we're working with a new business coaching client, for the first six months one area we focus on is upgrading the business owner's *personal* use of time; then we work to help the key team members upgrade their use of business time.

What we've found—and what you'll find when you apply these six simple time mastery strategies—is that you can create eight or more hours a week to reinvest in building your business. In fact, our coaching clients average a savings of *12 hours* a week, which they have free to redirect into other better and higher uses inside their business.

We're not asking you to work longer hours or nights or weekends. Far from it. Instead, we're asking that you consciously take charge of *how* you use your time, and focus it on the best and highest return for your business.

Before we share these six strategies with you, imagine for a moment that they worked. Don't you know that you could grow your business by 25 to 50 percent or more if you could just create an extra day or two each week to step back out of the job of your business to focus on taking those action steps that would grow and expand your business? Of course you could. That's why these strategies and techniques will make such an immediate and dramatic difference in your business.

---

6 TIME MASTERY STRATEGIES

Time Mastery Strategy #1: To upgrade your use of time, first identify what you do that truly creates value for your business.

Time Mastery Strategy #2: To "find" the time, focus first on your D level activities.

Time Mastery Strategy #3: Structure your week to take one "Focus Day" each week.

Time Mastery Strategy #4: Work "above the line" and live by the Results Rule™.

Time Mastery Strategy #5: Every "Push Day," schedule a 60-minute "Prime Time" block to work on A or B level activities.

Time Mastery Strategy #6: Create a "Stop Doing" List and add to it weekly.

Time Mastery Strategy #1

To upgrade your use of time, first identify what you do that truly creates value for your business.

As a business owner, you don't get paid for time and effort; you get paid for creating value. So as you build your business, look for ways to create value independently of putting in your personal time. This essentially is what it means to build a business, not a job.

If you've read anything on time management, you've come across Pareto's Principle, inspired by the work of 19th-century economist Vilfredo Pareto. Commonly called the 80–20 Rule, Pareto's Principle says that 20 percent of your actions generate 80 percent of your results (high value) and the other 80 percent of your actions generate the other 20 percent of your results (low value).

This useful distinction becomes the basis of a refined model for using your time to create massive value, independent of the hours you put in.

If you take the 20 percent of your actions that generate 80 percent of your results and apply the same distinction a second time, then 20 percent of that 20 percent produces 80 percent of 80 percent of your results. That means 4 percent of your effort (the 20 percent of 20 percent) generates 64 percent of your results.

And if you can bear with us for one more math moment, apply this distinction one final time.

This means that only 1 percent (20 percent of 20 percent of 20 percent) generates 50 percent of your results! That's right; only a fraction of your highest-leverage work produces *half* of all your results.

We used this idea to create something called the Time Value Matrix™— an actual formula to quickly and accurately quantify the per-hour value of four distinct types of time: A time, B time, C time, and D time, as shown in Figure 5.1. Also, we've included two hours of additional video training in the free Business Owner Tool Kit we've included with this book. To access these videos and dozens of other business growth tools simple visit **MauiMastermind.com/freetoolkit**. (See Appendix A for full details.)

D time is the 80 percent of unleveraged, wasteful time that produces only 20 percent of your total return. We call this the "80 Percent Mass."

C time is the leveraged 20 percent that produces 80 percent of your results. We call this "Leveraged Time."

B time is the highly focused 4 percent that generates 64 percent of your results. We call this time the "4 Percent Sweet Spot."

TIME VALUE MATRIX™

	INPUT	OUTPUT	RELATIVE VALUE
A *time* Magic 1%	1%	50%	200 XD
B *time* 4% Sweet Spot	4%	64%	64 XD
C *time* Leveraged 20%	20%	80%	16 XD
D *time* 80% Mass	80%	20%	1 XD

Figure 5.1: The Time Value Matrix
Copyright © Maui Mastermind®

A time is the top of the pyramid—the "Magic 1 Percent." Fully 50 percent of your results come from these activities.

Did you know that most business owners have no clue which of their activities fall into these four categories? So how in the world can you create more A and B time if you don't know what activities constitute A and B time for you?

Before we share with you some examples of our A-B-C-D level activities, understand that one person's D activity may be another person's A or B level activity—it's all relative. The examples from our business lives are illustrations that are not to be taken as absolute benchmarks of value. For example, one of David's D level activities is dealing with billing disputes. However, people in his company have this activity as one of their C or B level activities. Your A-B-C-D level activities are comparable only to you, not to other people.

Take action and examine what creates the highest value for your business at this moment in time.

Action Time: Identify your A-B-C-D activities and learn what you do that truly creates value for your business.

D Time: The 80 percent mass of unleveraged, wasteful time that produces only 20 percent of your total return.

Examples of David's D activities:

- Sorting mail
- Paying for and disputing bills
- Low-level email
- Scanning documents into his electronic filing system
- Setting up phone meetings

List five of your D activities.

1. _____
2. _____
3. _____
4. _____
5. _____

C Time: The leveraged 20 percent that produces 80 percent of your results. Examples of David's C activities:

- Delegating to his assistant
- Dictating a letter
- Holding a group meeting versus talking with several people one at a time
- Updating his master to-do list
- Sending out an email update to his executive team

List five of your C activities.

1. _____
2. _____
3. _____
4. _____
5. _____

B Time: The highly focused 4 percent "sweet spot" that generates 64 percent of your results.

Examples of Stephanie's B activities:

- Meeting with key clients to solidify the relationship
- Coaching her management team to be better leaders

- Sharing company stories, successes, and challenges in her biweekly letter that accompanies team members' paychecks
- Reviewing her company's quarterly progress
- Instituting a systemic solution to a recurring problem

List five of your B activities.

1. _____
2. _____
3. _____
4. _____
5. _____

A Time: The magic 1 percent that generates more than 50 percent of your total results.

Examples of David's A activities:

- Making executive-level hiring decisions
- Decision meetings with key joint venture partners to secure high-value, win-win strategic partnerships
- Making strategic decisions that set the direction of the business
- Holding the executive team accountable for their deliverables

List five of your A activities.

1. _____
2. _____
3. _____
4. _____
5. _____

Now that you've identified your current A-B-C-D level activities, it's important to understand that what you currently list as an A or B level activity will change. For example, if meeting one-on-one with a prospective client is an A level activity for you, make sure that in 6 to 12 months, you've increased the value you create for your business so this activity is pushed down to a B or C level activity. Ideally, working with a joint venture partner who can generate dozens of leads for you every month will become an A level activity, or training your sales team to meet with prospective clients one-to-one, or creating a sales video that generates passive sales. By that point, meeting one-to-one with a prospective client is no longer important for you to do personally. This is good. This is growth. And it's why your business becomes increasingly more valuable over time.

When you really get this distinction and shift your focus from putting in hours to *upgrading* the type of work you do (more A and B time and less D time), you'll find the results to be amazing.

Take the example of Dr. Gurpreet Padda, a physician who practices in St. Louis, Missouri. As you can imagine, like any successful medical professional, Dr. Padda's days are very full.

When we first started working with Dr. Padda nine years ago, he thought the highest use of his time was the time he spent in surgery, doing the pain-intervention spinal procedures at which he was a world-class expert. But the more he took these time mastery and business growth concepts to heart, the clearer it became that while very lucrative, these surgery hours were not his best and highest use for his companies; rather, the strategic decisions he made, the key hires he brought on board, and the crucial negotiations he engaged in were his real A and B level activities.

Here's how Dr. Padda put it: *"I'm a surgeon with a thriving pain management practice. At the time I first started using David's time mastery strategies I was already stretched to the maximum running a dozen different businesses, from a medical billing company to several commercial real estate projects and even a few restaurants. I knew time was my most precious resource but the insight that I had a higher order of time beyond my hours in surgery was a fresh one. These ideas helped me radically upgrade my use of time and within two years I increased my personal income by* an additional $1 million per year. *I still use these strategies and to this day find them just as useful and profitable."*

Clearly Dr. Padda is an outlier of just how effective these time mastery strategies can be when combined with the business growth principles and tactics you've learned earlier in this book. Today he owns 32 different businesses with more than 500 employees. He runs seven medical clinics, multiple restaurants, a microbrewery, and two organic farms.

Remember, it's limited, owner-reliant, Level Two thinking to believe that the solution is to work harder and longer. Instead, it's imperative that you upgrade your use of time. For example, if you were an attorney who charged $300 an hour, what would your D time activities be? Things like fixing a computer glitch, making copies, sorting mail, or other little things for which you can't bill a client. And what would your

C time activities be? Any time that's billable, like working on a legal brief, reviewing a contract, or updating a client on legal considerations.

Understand this: C time can provide you with a great income, but you'll always have to work exceptionally hard to earn it and it will likely be dependent on your personal participation. This is the trap that catches most high-income professionals. They seek to increase their earnings by cranking out more hours. Mistake! Working more hours will take you only so far; it's just not scalable past a certain point (not to mention that when you get there, you'll be exhausted from so much work and a stranger to your family, too).

The answer lies in A and B time. For an attorney, B time might include building relationships with other professionals who can refer valuable business, or putting systems in place so staff can get better results without tapping too much into the attorney's time.

What would A time look like? This could be speaking at a large conference where this attorney is able to generate new client relationships worth hundreds of thousands or even millions of dollars in billable services. Or it might be creating an accounts receivable system that increases the collection on all the firm's billings by 10 percent.

See the difference? You want to get D level activities off your plate; C time is needed to do your work more effectively. A and B time, however, are when you step out of the "job" of the work and do something that improves your capacity to create results, or significantly pushes back your biggest limiting factor (e.g., generating new clients, improving a critical system, etc.).

In fact, by upgrading your use of time instead of increasing your hours worked, you can often create huge business breakthroughs while still working fewer hours. Trading time for dollars is a Level Two reaction. Upgrading your use of time to create more with less is the Level Three solution.

So here's the big question: *How can you have more A and B time?* You won't get it by trying harder or by sitting down and saying, *"Okay, let's have an A moment right now."* Sorry, it just doesn't work that way. That would be like a parent saying to a three-year-old, *"Let's have an hour of quality time right now, Junior."* How well do you think that would work?

To get more A and B time, you have to fundamentally alter the way you *structure* your day and your week, which is exactly what the next four time mastery strategies will help you do.

Time Mastery Strategy #2

To "find" the time, focus first on your D level activities.

This one may seem counterintuitive, but the best place to look *first* to upgrade your use of time isn't your A, B, or C level activities. It's looking at your D level activities. Not only by definition do you spend a lot more time at this level, but it's the easiest place to make changes because the consequences of dropping those activities are small.

So list all the D level activities you do on a weekly basis. Even keep a time log for a week or two so you can spot the wasted time spent on low-value D activities. Once you've identified them, you can apply the following "four Ds" to get them off your plate.

The Four Ds

1. **Delete it.** Some D activities just plain shouldn't be done by anyone. Look at the action item and ask yourself what would be the consequences if no one did it. If the consequences would be small, then consider just crossing it off of your list altogether.

2. **Delegate it.** Maybe it's a task that needs to get done, but not necessarily by *you*. Hand it off to your assistant, or a staff member, or a vendor. Anytime you can hand off a D level activity to someone, you free up both your time and your focus to do more valuable work for your business. (Make sure you watch the training video included in the Business Owner Tool Kit, which you get as part of this book, for a short video on how to find, hire, and leverage your personal assistant. Go to **www.MauiMastermind.com/freetoolkit** for instant access.)

3. **Defer it.** Maybe this task needs to be done and done by you, but should it happen right now? Sometimes delaying the action is the smartest choice.

4. **Design it out.** If you find yourself handling a recurring D activity over and over, instead of doing it, improve the process or system to keep the task from coming up in the first place. For example, if you get the same seven customer questions repeatedly, post a FAQ page with the answers on your website. Or perhaps you can preempt questions by giving new clients a "quick start" booklet that proactively answers these seven questions. Or maybe post an instructional video on your website that gives new clients your best presentation while answering these common questions. You

get the idea. Designing out a recurring activity is the very essence of building a systems-reliant Level Three business. It simplifies processes and empowers your team to get consistently great results with less and less reliance on you, the business owner.

So after you've identified what you do that truly creates value (your A and B activities), look closely at your D activities as the place to mine the raw ore of more time. By applying the four Ds of Deleting, Delegating, Deferring, and Designing Out, you'll free up eight or more hours each week to reinvest in A and B activities. When you upgrade your time, you'll increase your sales, improve your cash flow, and dramatically grow your business.

Time Mastery Strategy #3

Structure your week to take one "Focus Day" each week.
It's not enough to free up eight to 10 hours each week by clearing the clutter of your D activities; you have to fill your freed-up time with A and B activities. Nature abhors a vacuum, and if you don't fundamentally change how you structure your week, you'll find yourself squandering the time you supposedly saved on more D level junk.

Action Step: Set aside one Focus Day every week. On your Focus Day, get outside of your normal environment and work on the highest-leverage, highest-value, highest-return part of your business. Do the A and B level activities that add real value.

This could mean building out a baseline operational process to use with new clients. Or you could spend three hours creating a hiring system to help you consistently hire star staff members. Or you might call on your two most important prospective customers or joint venture partners to close the sale or deepen the relationship.

The key is to set aside a day a week (or at the very least *half* a day a week) as your Focus Day and make sure your team and environment support you in keeping this time clear so you can invest in these high-value A or B level activities.

Decision Time: What day will you make your Focus Day?

"My Focus Day will be _____."

DAVID'S STORY

Let me share a powerful concept to get more A and B time and minimize the D time that gets in the way. I call this technique Focus Days and Push Days.

Mondays, Wednesdays, and Fridays are my Push Days. These are the days that I push key projects forward step by step. That's when I'm accessible by phone and email, and I hold many of my phone meetings. It's when I get the "job" of my business done.

Then I set aside my Tuesdays and Thursdays for my Focus Days. That's when I turn off the phones and email for the majority of the day, and focus on doing the highest-value activities I can for my businesses (my A and B level activities). For me that usually involves writing: writing new books, writing new training tools for our business coaching system, or writing business plans for my teams to implement. It can also involve holding high-value meetings or being in the studio recording a new business growth training course.

On my Focus Days, I often leave the office and work remotely. Sometimes I go to a café or library and work there. Getting out of my normal environment removes the temptation to do the C and D level work that lives in every corner of my office. I also put an away message on my email and empower my assistant to screen my calls and handle or delay any of my emails. This frees me up to fully focus on my most valuable activities.

The most important part of what my Focus Days do is give me *blocks* of time. I've learned that to create my highest value for my business I need blocks of time. But, like most business owners, if I'm passive about how I structure my week, my time is fractured into small slivers—10 minutes here, five minutes there. Focus Days give me a base of consistent blocks of time in which to get my highest value activities done.

Here's the most amazing part. Three to four hours on my Focus Day can result in more value to my business than an *entire week* living in C or D level activities. Focus Days give you a way to create the space in which to get high-value work done. (In case you're wondering, I do check in for 30 to 45 minutes at the end of the day to answer important phone messages or emails.)

Perhaps you can't set aside two full days a week as Focus Days, but you *can* find one day (or at least *half* a day) every week and use it as your Focus Day.

Time Mastery Strategy #4

Every "Push Day," schedule a 60-minute "Prime Time" block to work on A or B activities.

Everyone has a certain time in the day when they're at their best. A Prime Time block is a 60-minute appointment that you set for yourself for your peak effectiveness time. That's when you work only on your highest-value items. By blocking out this time as an actual appointment on your calendar, you guarantee yourself at least one hour each Push Day to have a focused block of time to create real value for your business.

DAVID'S STORY

For me, I make my Prime Time in the morning from approximately 8:30 until 9:30 every Monday, Wednesday, and Friday, which are my Push Days. I accept no inbound phone calls or emails during my Prime Time unless I deem that email or phone call to be the highest use of my time.

Certainly I'm not perfect, and at times I struggle with this strategy, especially because of the urgency and seductiveness of email. But when I stay on target (currently about 75 percent of the time), it makes a huge difference in the value I get from my day. You'll find that setting aside this regular appointment to do your highest-value work allows you to create more value for your business.

Time Mastery Strategy #5

On your Push Days, work "above the line" and live by the Results Rule™.

Most business owners start each day with high hopes. They take a moment to write down the list of tasks for that day—a list that often grows to 15 or 20 items. But then the day hits and they find themselves pulled off track to deal with customer challenges, operational fires, or sales emergencies.

Here is a different way to organize each day.

When you sit down in the morning (or the night before, if you prefer), choose three "big rocks" for that day and write them at the top of your to-do list. Draw a line under them to visually mark them as different and special. Make two of them business related and one of them personal.

Your big rocks are the action steps you'll take that day that will create the most value for your business. Almost always these are A and B level activities. Here is an example of a time mastery to-do list.

SAMPLE TIME MASTERY TO-DO LIST

1. Draft the marketing calendar for Q1.

2. Call Tom Smith about expanding joint venture.

3. Write my wife a love letter.

Email Shirley.

Check on Collin's project status with Angela.

Review web PPC proposal.

Call Larry (webinar glitches).

Call Jenna (her event questions).

Etc.

Live by the Results Rule™

By 10:30 A.M., you should have either completed each of your three big rocks or have scheduled a definite appointment time to complete them. We call this the Results Rule. This technique is powerful because it pushes you to do what matters most *first*.

Most business owners put off these big rocks to deal with the urgent requests that come at them during the day. In doing so, they sacrifice far more than they'll ever know.

Time Mastery Strategy #6

Create a "Stop Doing" List and add to it weekly.

Too many people live their lives based on a to-do list to which they keep adding more and more tasks. But they rarely make the hard choices of what to let go of, what to delay, what to delegate, and what to delete altogether.

Look at your to-do lists from the past 60 days. Which activities can you add to your "Stop Doing" List, and how much time will that save you? Each week, pick a few more activities you deliberately choose to add to your "Stop Doing" List. You'll find that the items you put on it tend to be tasks you find draining—maybe ones you put on your to-do list out of obligation or inertia. When you get rid of them, you'll enjoy a sense of elation and energy plus have a much higher performance level in your other time.

The Real Secret to Unshakable Time Discipline

Most people shudder when thinking about a need for greater discipline, because they've always associated it with pain and effort. But this isn't accurate. Instead, we suggest that you link discipline to two very important concepts: accountability and environment.

Discipline Is One Part Accountability

There is a powerful drive in human nature that wants to be esteemed by those people you admire. One of the best ways to increase your time discipline is to have a formal accountability structure to someone whose respect you want to earn, and whose opinion of you matters greatly to you. This could be a formal business coach, an informal board of directors, or even your leadership team.

Whom do you turn to who will hold you accountable for your actions and decisions within your business? Who coaches you to help you develop as a business owner? Who helps keep you on track? If you want to build an owner-independent Level Three business, it's vital to have an accountability structure. And you need this accountability to be *formal*, not ad hoc, hit or miss. Formal means you make regular, timed commitments (e.g., weekly, biweekly, monthly, quarterly), with a structured way in which you report on your results meeting those commitments. No hiding is possible, just the naked truth that you stand up and own, unflinchingly. This one ingredient is perhaps the biggest reason David's business coaching clients grow on average at an annual rate nine times greater than the average privately held company in the United States— they have a structured accountability system that makes it impossible to hide.

What person do you turn to who will hold you accountable for your actions and decisions within your business? Who coaches you to help you develop as a business owner? Who helps keep you on track? If you want to build an owner-independent Level Three business, it's vital to have an accountability structure.

Remember, on your own, you are vulnerable; but connected with a peer group and advisor team who can give you feedback and accountability, you are unstoppable.

Discipline Is One Part Environment

Discipline also results from working in a structured environment. By controlling your environment, you make healthy, profitable behaviors for your business much easier. Remember, will power can win a sprint, but rarely a marathon. To win the marathon of building a Level Three business, take control of your environment to ensure it supports your goals each day. This means eliminating distractions on your Focus Days and during your Prime Time.

DAVID'S STORY

I happen to be a chocoholic. I love chocolate anything. If chocolate cake, ice cream, or cookies lurk anywhere in my house, I eat them up. So how have I learned to structure my environment to support my health goals? Simple. I don't bring chocolate into my home. I don't allow it. If it's not there to tempt me, then it's much easier for me to maintain my health goals. I rarely bring any food into my home that isn't healthy.

The same lesson of discipline applies to my business. As mentioned earlier, I use Tuesdays and Thursdays for my Focus Days. I've learned that if I stay in my office for my Focus Days, I'm tempted to do C and D activities. That's why I usually step into a conference room or head out to a café or library to work. Because I've controlled my environment to make distractions unlikely, it's almost impossible to get sidetracked by an interruption on my Focus Days.

The bottom line is that the real secret of time discipline is to harness the power of accountability (and the social drive we all have to be esteemed by people we respect) and to control your environment so that you design out those old distractions, at least for part of your week, and create a workspace that supports you working at your best.

In the next chapter we examine the four most costly business excuses that trap the average business owner in the daily ground and endless loop of the Self-Employment Trap.

CHAPTER 6

The 4 Most Costly Excuses That Hold Business Owners Back

What do you think stops you from taking your business to the next level? The daily demands of one crisis after another crashing down on you? A lack of cash to grow your company? Outside forces like a tough economy or governmental regulation?

Ask yourself this question: *What have been the real excuses I've accepted in my past that have kept me from reaching my goals?*

Over the past decade, we've helped more than 100,000 business owners make their businesses more successful and less owner reliant. During this extended time, a distinct pattern has emerged about what it *really* takes to build a thriving owner-independent business. Here are the four biggest excuses that we've observed have held other business owners back and why we think they simply no longer serve you. It's a strange phenomenon we've repeatedly observed wherein smart, capable, and committed business owners stridently argue for the very limitations that are what hold them back from enjoying an extraordinary quality of life and business success. Remember, in life if you argue for your excuses you get to keep them.

This chapter candidly explores these four major excuses and empowers you to let them go. Business owners who've gone on to enjoy the wealthiest lives (financially and otherwise) have *all* found ways to take responsibility for their business lives and let go of these costly excuses. Now it's your turn to do the same.

Excuse #1: "I can't afford it . . ."

Whether you think you can't afford the lost production if you were to claim back two to four hours a week to focus on higher-order activities, or that you can't afford the outside help to implement and execute on the Level Three Map in a disciplined, effective manner, or that somehow applying the formula laid out in this book is going to push you to make hires sooner than you can afford them, the money excuse is more smoke than substance.

Most business owners think only in terms of what it will cost them to invest in the staff, or the systems, or the education, or the outside help they need to grow and develop their companies. For them, the decision is skewed because they only look at the cost of doing this new behavior or executing on this new decision or strategy. What they ignore is the true cost of the status quo.

Let's revisit the example of Bruce, the surgeon whose story we shared with you in Chapter 1. Like so many other business owners, Bruce was so mired in being a producer for his business that he wasn't able to step back and see his business accurately. For him being a producer meant seeing patients and doing surgical procedures. One of the first things he discovered when he started in the business coaching pro- gram was that one part of his medical practice, his medical spa, was losing quite a bit of money every year. Not only was this part of the practice stressful and time intensive for his staff, but Bruce was actually *paying* to keep it going. In fact, his status quo was costing him $70,000 of direct costs, plus tens of thousands of dollars more of hidden, indirect staff costs. This is a clear example of what we mean when we tell business owners that the cost of the status quo is already much higher than the minimal cost to get started maturing and progressing their companies to Level Three.

Not only was the net effect on Bruce's practice of converting that $70,000 annual loss into a $200,000 annual gain the equivalent of $270,000 a year of additional profit for his practice, but, more impor- tant, he has given him- self the breathing room to see his practice from a better vantage point. In his case this has allowed him to finally bring on another surgeon and create a concrete pathway to continue to scale his practice. He's grown his profits and reduced his working hours by 10 hours a week. Here's how Bruce describes this change:

"I had 12 years of advanced medical training to become a surgeon, yet I received no training about how to run a successful medical practice. I had to learn by trial and error. Now, with the support and training

of my business coach, I'm finally getting that business training. It's just been six months since I started this work but already we've fixed one part of our practice that was a medical spa, turning what was a $70,000-a-year loss into a $200,000-a-year profit center. I've found a part-time surgeon to complement me in the practice, and am on a pathway to grow her participation in the practice, which is also giving me a proven model to bring other surgeons onto our team over the coming years. I'm working fewer hours, and actually getting home before the sun sets, which is a real gift. Best of all, I can see the practice becoming stronger and less reliant on me bit by bit each quarter."

Bruce's story is not unusual. Blake Schwank. Blake served 11 years' active duty in the U.S. Army. After Blake separated from the military, he took that leadership and technology training with him and put it to use, founding an IT services company in Colorado Springs. He slowly grew that company to a $450,000-a-year Middle Stage Level Two business. The company worked, but only because Blake was there each day making sure it worked. He was the company's lead IT tech, and then at nights and on weekends he would do the admin, bookkeeping, and invoicing that he didn't have time to do during the workday.

In 2009 Blake began working with David's business coaching company. After doing the initial "audit" that every new coaching client goes through, Blake's business coach pointed out that he had $60,000 of accounts receivable that had gone uncollected for more than a year, and that this problem was getting worse as it compounded itself every month due to the glaring holes in his collections system.

At first Blake, like most business owners, wanted to rationalize and explain away this issue. But his coach wouldn't let him off that easily and pushed him to address the underlying issue. Once Blake fixed this broken system, his company immediately gained over $75,000 a year of additional operating profit. Remember, all of Blake's expenses were *already being paid*, so this additional money that he now collected dropped straight to his bottom line. This money was his to keep as additional profit, or money that could be reinvested back into his company to help it grow. In Blake's case he did both, keeping some of the extra profit and reinvesting a portion of it back to help him scale to 29 team members and over $3 million per year in sales.

Our point is this: When we hear business owners say they can't afford to follow what we've shared in this book to progress their businesses, we know that they are just leaning on an easy excuse. And this excuse is actually one of the biggest problems holding them back. They are likely not seeing some way that their status quo is already costing them tens or even hundreds of thousands of dollars every year, whether that cost be the lost profit from a broken area of the business they were ignoring like it was for Bruce, or the opportunity cost of lost growth like it was for Blake until he fixed his collections system and freed up profit for him to reinvest back into his company to grow it 600 percent.

You *can* afford to grow your business and get your life back; you just have to make the decision to do it. It rarely if ever requires outside capital, and almost always can be accomplished by conducting your core business just a little bit better and smarter.

Excuse #2: "I don't have the time . . ."

No business owner ever initially feels like he or she has extra time to scale his or her company. On the whole, business owners feel maxed out and strained to capacity. We've invested much of this book explaining the reason why.

But let's be clear—you don't need to work any more hours. We're not asking you to work nights or weekends. All we are asking is that at a minimum you take one Focus Day (or half a day—or half of half a day!) each week to invest in your higher-order activities for your company. When you use this two- to four-hour block of time you take each week as a wedge, it will drive home the opening you need to start progressing your business.

Klayton owned a retail store with sales of $750,000. The business was profitable, and supported his family (wife and two young kids) well. But Klayton was also working 70 hours a week, which kept him at the store working on the showroom floor or in the office overseeing the operations of the business, instead being home playing with his kids. If Klayton had kept on saying, *"I don't have the time to apply any of these ideas to grow my company,"* where would he be today? An easy question—he'd still be working 70 hours a week running a successful but exhausting owner-reliant retail store. His kids would be getting older, and just taking it for granted that *"Dad just works all the time—that's why we never see him."* But Klayton didn't let his lack of time stop him from making the necessary changes to his business. He pushed himself to carve out just a few hours a week to follow the plan of action that he and his business coach mapped out each quarter. He built his system, developed his team, and slowly weaned his business off of its total dependence on him. And where is he today, four years later?

Today Klayton's company has two retail locations doing $1.5 million per year in sales. Plus, he opened up a commercial division that is doing another $2 million per year in brand-new business, for total sales today of $3.5 million—367 percent bigger and more profitable than four years earlier.

And what about his work hours? Is he still putting in what is almost the equivalent of two full-time jobs working 70 hours a week? Far from it. He has cut his working hours in half to under 35 hours a week. Plus, on the ad- vice of his business coach, he's taking at least one week of vacation every quarter, something that he never used to do. The bottom line is that Klayton has literally halved his working day and almost qua-drupled his sales and profits. Still, there are going to be a few business owners who insist they "don't have the time" to apply even a few of the ideas that they learned.

Remember, you don't have to do this all at once. You just need to start now, here, today, and make small changes. With those small changes in producing for your company, you'll be able to expand and build on these successes to invest a bit more of your time. You'll build more sys-tems and delegate better to your team, which in turn will free up even more of your time. Eventually you'll reach the point where most of the day-to-day operations of your business will rely on other people using your company's systems and controls. Remember, this is a progression, not an on/off switch. You just have to get started now.

Excuse #3: "I'm overwhelmed . . ."

This is a more raw, honest version of excuse number two. What these business owners are really saying is, *"I don't know where to start. I feel out of control."* They are feeling so pressured with keeping their heads above water meeting all the demands on their time and day that they can't see past the next wave about to come crashing down on their heads. For these business owners, it feels like everyone wants a piece of them. It feels like they are being picked apart daily, one request at a time.

Here's the good news: It has been our direct experience coaching hundreds of business owners to execute on the ideas and strategies explained in this book that if you are serious about making things bet-ter, you can see a sizable shift in a very short time. A quick review of David's business coaching clients shows that the norm is that within 180 days of getting started on this path to Level Three you'll feel like you can breathe again, like you're the one in control of your business versus your business controlling you.

RC came with his parents to the United States from Mexico. His family was close and loving, but very poor. As a kid RC worked with his mom and dad picking produce in the hot, dusty fields of central California. As he grew up, he was driven to succeed. In college, which is where he met his wife Dalia, he read his first book on business and began to creatively buy investment real estate. After college, he and Dalia were married and worked to scale their fledgling real estate company. It was about this time that RC first learned about David's work, and attended several of his company's workshops. The ideas he learned were like water on parched earth—RC just drank them up. He was in his mid-twenties by this time and hungry to grow and succeed.

And grow he did. His company expanded quickly. RC was at the helm of a buying juggernaut, buying, fixing up, and reselling or renting out hundreds of single-family homes over the next few years. With Dalia firmly in control of the office, keeping a close eye on their finances and contracts, the business flourished. They were earning a seven-figure annual profit, but this profit came at a cost: RC was *always* working.

A typical day would have him working in the office from 8 A.M. to 7 P.M., and then there was "the phone," as Dalia called it. The phone: such a powerful tool for getting work done, but for Dalia, that phone had be- come a symbol of how her husband was always working. At night and on weekends contractors would call with construction questions, vendors would call with pricing or payment challenges, staff would call with operational questions, and prospects would call with potential new opportunities of homes to buy or sell. And RC was there to take each of these calls. He was a prisoner of his own competence because for years he had built his company to leverage his talents. It revolved around him—his decisions, his directions, his negotiations, his production.

Something needed to change. By the time RC reached out again to David's company to get more direct coaching versus taking the DIY route, he and Dalia had two young children. In some ways Dalia was just resigned that this was the way life would be. It wasn't so bad, she reasoned to herself. She had a husband whom she loved who was totally committed to his family. The business gave them the financial security that neither of them had ever dreamed possible. It was just that RC worked, and worked, and worked.

When RC first told Dalia that he wanted to join David's business coaching program so he could stop working so many hours, Dalia was skeptical. It wasn't that she felt the program wouldn't work; it was just that she doubted her husband's resolve to actually stop working so many hours. But when she thought about it, she realized she had nothing to lose. It wasn't as if RC could work any *more* hours, so she gave her blessing.

At first the progress was small, almost impossible to see. The first quarter in the program, RC and Dalia worked with their business coach to tackle their capital-raising part of the business. Together they found a better way to reduce their cost of capital by half a million dollars a year. While this meant half a million dollars of additional profit, the most amazing thing about this was that these changes gave RC back five hours a week of his time. They hadn't realized how time intensive it was for him to constantly be cultivating and developing their private investor base.

With this newfound time, they spent the next quarter working to make some leveraged changes to their core operations, engaging their team for the first time in really "owning" parts of the business, versus just being the hands that RC directed. This also gave RC back a little more of his time. With his coach holding him accountable, he started to leave the office at 4:30 or 5:00 P.M. each day, getting home to have dinner with his family most nights during the week.

But still there was "the phone." It rang during meals, late at night, and even on weekends. And each time it rang it pulled RC away from Dalia and his family and into the world of the business.

Then in the final quarter of his first year working with his Maui coach, RC finally felt ready to tackle the phone. They charted out the specific types of calls he got on the phone and where these calls came from. They calculated the value of each of these calls, and who on his team could, along with some training and tools, handle these types of calls. They figured out how they could systematically redirect each of the main call sources so they never reached RC's cell phone in the first place, and over an eight-week period they implemented their plan. And it worked! Through the work he had done to strengthen the business—its systems, team, and culture—along with the new habits he'd gained through his focused work with his Maui business coach, RC was able to let go of 90 percent of the calls.

"I never thought I'd see the day when he'd be home with us and ignore his phone," Dalia shared. *"But it's happened. He's now working so much less, and when he's home, he's really there with us."*

RC put it this way: *"It was just time. I had worked so hard all those years to get to the point where the business was thriving, but I just didn't see the impact of all those calls on Dalia and my kids. When I started in the program it really helped me see that impact, which gave me the motivation to make things better. What's amazing to me is how quickly this has all happened. It's been less than a year in the program and my company is more profitable than ever. We've driven our cost of capital down by half a million dollars or more, my team is fully on board in this process, and I have so much more time with my family. What the program has shown me is that I could build the business to be more owner independent. I just needed a structured map and the accountability to do it differently. My only regret is that I didn't get started in the program sooner."*

Excuse #4: "Now's just not the right time . . ."

This is the business owner who says, *"Stephanie, David, I totally see it. I'm right here on board with all that you've shared in the book, but the timing is just not quite right."*

What this person doesn't realize is how expensive that statement is in terms of lost profits and lost time freedom. In fact, in our experience this fourth excuse is the most damaging and dangerous one of all. In effect, excuse number four says, *"Hey, someday the time will be just right, and at that perfect time—and only then—I'll take that first step to use what you've shared with me."*

It's as if this business owner says that he'll wait until someday when he's magically cleared his calendar or gotten past the current fire he is dealing with, and then he'll do the things that will make the business less reliant on him. Yet sadly this someday never comes.

Instead you've got to make the decision that your someday is now, and that your starting point is today. The reality is that the timing will never be just right, for this or for anything. Now is the only time you have to get started. Today is the only day to make a new beginning so you can enjoy a better ending. In the words of Nike, *"Just do it!"*

Ask any of the business owners we worked with for inclusion in this book what would have happened to their companies if they had waited until all the stars were in perfect alignment before starting on this work. All of them would tell you that waiting would have only made things worse. The fact that they had the courage to start, even with things being chaotic, hectic, or messy in their companies, was the one trait they had in common. And it let them enjoy life-changing results, including increased sales, improved profit margins, stronger businesses, and greater owner freedom.

In the final chapter, we'll walk you through four simple action steps to turn the ideas in this book into concrete results for your business.

CHAPTER 7

4 Simple Action Steps to Get Started Now

Congratulations! You've made it to the final chapter—a real accomplishment. You've not only invested the time to read the rich array of business-building strategies and concepts we've shared, but more important, you've embraced the vision of building an owner-independent Level Three business.

Now it's time for you to step up and apply what you've learned to take your business to the next level. In this final chapter, you'll discover four simple steps for you to take immediately to apply what you've learned in this book to accelerate your progress to Level Three.

Action Step #1: Make building an owner-independent Level Three company a stated goal of your business.

On May 25, 1961, in a speech before a joint session of Congress, President John F. Kennedy set out a bold goal: *"I believe that this nation should commit itself to achieving the goal, before this decade is out, of landing a man on the moon and returning him safely to the earth."* This commitment galvanized the United States in a decade-long race that culminated on July 20, 1969, with Neil Armstrong and Buzz Aldrin landing on the moon.

Are we saying that the goal of building an owner-independent company is the business equivalent of a moon shot? Far from it. But a combined 50 years in business has taught us both to respect and harness the power of a clearly articulated and shared vision inside an organization. That's why we are coaching you that your first step after putting this book down is to make building an owner-independent Level Three business a stated goal within your company.

When your team understands that this is important for their future, in terms of increased job security and greater opportunities to contribute and earn, they will slowly start to buy into this shared vision.

This isn't an overnight move but a longer-term commitment. Review your "why's" for building an owner-independent company that you wrote down at the very end of Chapter 1. Whose lives will your company touch by holding true to your Level Three vision? Remember, your purpose needs to extend beyond just making more money. Your business must support your deeper values. How will owning a Level Three business impact your family? Your employees? Your community? How will it allow you to give more money and time to causes you care deeply about? How will you be an inspiration to others? We grow wealthy by what we give. How will you share your good fortune on a bigger playing field? Remember, you can never really pay it back, but you can pay it forward.

Next you need to help each of your team members articulate their deeper why's for being part of this journey with the company. How does building a Level Three company support their larger life goals in some meaningful way?

When you are all working toward one common end, you will marvel at the heights you can collectively reach.

Action Step #2: Claim back some of your best time by taking one Focus Day each week.

Start small and build from there. While you can't control your full week, you can claim back at least two to four hours one day each week as your Focus Day. If you're able, make this a six-hour block, but at the very least, reclaim two hours a week in which to focus on your A and B level activities that truly create value for your business.

Put this time as a definite appointment on your calendar. You wouldn't be so rude as to stand up someone you had a meeting with, so treat your Focus Day appointment with the same degree of respect. Don't stand up yourself and your business.

We believe that once you see the cumulative power of these precious blocks of time, you'll become hooked and follow our other time mastery suggestions, including taking a Prime Time block of time each Push Day for an additional one hour a day. But at the very least we know you can take a two- to four-hour Focus Day block each week, and this time will be the starting point for progressing your business.

Action Step #3: Get a business coach.

All top athletes have an experienced coach, and so do many of the world's most successful entrepreneurs. Your coach's job is to help push you to perform at your best, and help you avoid the expensive trial and error that most business owners take as they build a business.

It's hard for you to gain the perspective you need to see your company and your behavior as a leader of your company with the necessary clarity to take your business to the next level. This is what the right business coach will do for you. He or she will push you, challenge you, support you, and guide you.

The right coach will hold you accountable in a structured, programmatic way. Remember, when you're looking for the right coaching fit, pick a coaching *program*, not just a coach. It has been our experience that the right coaching program makes sure that your coach balances your company's immediate day-to-day operational needs with its longer-term development strategy. If your coach just helps you deal with your current challenges but doesn't give you a clear map to consistently reduce your company's reliance on you by enhancing its systems, team, controls, and culture, you just may end up more firmly trapped in an owner-reliant Level Two business.

In fact, we'll go one better. If building an owner-independent Level Three company isn't a stated goal and structural objective of the coaching program you are considering, don't join. Find a company that has the right mix of coaching magic and program structure and experience to accelerate you to Level Three.

Action Step #4: Start now!

The final action step is to simply get started—now—today. The time will never be just right. Any delay just costs you momentum. So just jump in and get started.

You don't need a perfect start; you just need to get moving. You'll figure out refinements and learn lessons along the way. But you need to get started now.

You Can Do It, and the Rewards Are Worth the Effort

Patrice and her husband Rob ran a large medical education company, hosting over 100 medical conferences for 10,000 primary care physicians each year. The company had progressed, but Patrice still felt compelled to work long hours, well past the point when the business really needed her to do this.

"I was working an average of 80 hours or more each week," Patrice shared. *"Rob and I did take vacation time, but we did conference calls, worked on content development for future conferences, and handled staff issues when away. If I were being honest about it, our vacations were re- ally more like working remotely. Sure,*

the locations were pretty, but the fact that we still felt so tied to the business really pointed out a flaw in how we were growing the company. It was at one of David's business conferences when Rob and I had an 'aha' moment. We realized that part of owning a successful business meant that it had to be owner independent, and that the biggest thing holding back our company from reaching this threshold was ourselves."

So Patrice and Rob and their third partner made the concrete decision to take their company to Level Three. That meant leaning more heavily on their staff and trusting them to own more in the business. They also got more strategic about which parts of the business to invest more in, and which to step away from. They freed up their time by leveraging their systems, team, and culture, which allowed Patrice, Rob, and their third partner to focus on their fewer, more important activities and decisions.

The end result was a business that was more profitable, more sustainable, and more enjoyable to own. *"We now work 20 to 30 hours a week, enjoy eight weeks of real vacation each year, and earn far more income."* Or listen to the story of Jake, owner of a small private equity firm that specializes in the purchase of distressed assets like commercial mort- gages, failed development projects, or struggling commercial real estate. Jake is bright, focused, and, from the start, very talented at what he does. Perhaps this was one of his problems. Like so many business owners before him, he found that the fastest way to grow his business was to do more of what he was very good at doing. For him that meant sourcing more deals, doing the deep due diligence, and raising more capital to close on these acquisitions. But the more deals he personally tried to do, the more the business relied on his production. This led him into the trap of longer hours and less time away from the business.

In fact, in 2012, shortly after the birth of his daughter, Jake was working 80 hours a week to finish raising the capital to close a key deal he had under contract. During that time there were days when Jake would leave before his wife or daughter woke up, only to return home long after they had gone to bed. *"Looking back,"* Jake shared, *"I feel so sad that I missed more time with them during that period of my company. At the time I just didn't know how to do it any differently."*

Since that time Jake has been following the same steps you've learned in this book to grow his company by increasing its owner independence. Working with his Maui business coach, Jake's firm has increased its deal volume from $3 million its first year to $55 million in deals last year. At the same time its "gross promote," the private equity equivalent of gross profit, has grown from just under half a million dollars a year to over

$8.5 million. How was he able to create and sustain this kind of growth? By following the same steps you've learned in this book to develop his team, formalize and refine his systems, implement smart internal controls, and build a culture wherein the entire company was engaged in finding, funding, and executing on profitable deals.

"So much has changed now," Jake reported. *"In fact, we've done multiple deals this past year where we raised more money than that earlier deal. The thing that's different is that now I've got a team, systems, and company culture that help us do it. I now average 40 to 50 hours a week, which is a magnitude less than back in 2012. I also take more time away from the business. I am so glad I invested the time, money, and energy to apply these concepts to progress on our goal of building an owner-independent company."*

If you were to ask Patrice or Jake at the start of their Level Three journey if they ever thought they would succeed the way they have done, they would tell you that they struggled with the same doubts and fears you do. Remember, feeling afraid is normal when you're stretching yourself and going after your dreams. It's a sign that you're growing.

If you ever doubt your capacity to stay the course and reach Level Three, then borrow *our* faith. *We* know you can do it. And you're not alone. Thousands of other business owners in the Maui Mastermind community stand by your side. Together, we can support each other and accomplish our goals. The world needs you to embrace your power and live your dreams.

You'll never have the chance to relive this moment, so make it count. Thank you for letting us play a part in your progression to build an owner-independent company. Enjoy your journey to Level Three—it is worth the investment of time, energy, and money. Build a business you love owning and get your life back.

David and Stephanie

ABOUT THE AUTHORS

David Finkel is an ex-Olympic-level athlete turned business multimillionaire and is one of the nation's most respected business thinkers. A *Wall Street Journal* and *BusinessWeek* bestselling author of 10 business books, including coauthor of *SCALE: Seven Proven Principles to Grow Your Business and Get Your Life Back*, with Priceline.com cofounder Jeff Hoffman.

David is the founder and CEO of Maui Mastermind® (**www.MauiMastermind.com**), one of the world's premier business coaching companies, which has worked with more than 100,000 business owners, helping them grow their companies and get their lives back. David's business coaching clients enjoy an average annual growth rate five times higher than the average privately held company in the United States, while at the same time increasing their companies' "Owner Independence" by an average of 97.4 percent per year. Over the past 20 years, David and the other Maui coaches and advisors have personally scaled companies with an aggregate market value of $63 billion. Millions of business owners get his weekly e-letter, listen to his podcast (The Business Coach), or have read his syndicated column in Inc.com. His work has been featured in such prestigious media outlets as the *Wall Street Journal, International Business Times, Bloomberg Businessweek,* Fox Business, MSNBC, and *Inc.* magazine.

An in-demand keynote speaker, David's message of how to grow a business by strengthening its core systems, team, and culture has galvanized business audiences around the globe.

He and his wife Heather and their three sons live in Jackson Hole, Wyoming. David eats his own cooking, growing and maturing his business wile taking five months off each year.

Stephanie Harkness has been a serial entrepreneur for more than 35 years, with eight successful businesses under her direct leadership. For 25 years, her primary focus was JunoPacific, which runs a 24/7 operation serving the medical device and life sciences markets where precision engineering, short lead times, and class 1000 cleanrooms are required by exacting customer requirements to support FDA contract manufacturing and assembly.

Co-owned with her husband Jack, their company, with 300 employees, shepherded more than 100 start-ups through funding by venture capitalists with the expected outcome of acquisition or IPO. She led in the development of their corporate boards and executive teams. The majority of customers were successful in raising capital, building products for FDA approval, and securing a successful outcome for shareholders.

Five years ago Stephanie and Jack sold this thriving company to a private manufacturing enterprise focused on growing its presence in Silicon Valley by having the top brand in the country for medical device projects in its portfolio.

Stephanie's past awards include the Freedom Award presented by the National Association of Manufacturers (two other recipients have been Ronald Reagan and Henry Ford), and #5 in the *Business Journal* Top 50 Women Business Owners in California; she was named Customer of the Year and featured in Wells Fargo Bank's Annual Shareholder Report, as well as National Woman Business Owner.

A former client of Maui Mastermind, Stephanie has volunteered as a Maui Advisor since 2007, paying it forward to other business owners and helping them make their businesses more successful.

THE BUSINESS OWNER TOOL KIT—YOUR <u>FREE</u> $1,375 GIFT FROM THE AUTHORS

Dear Reader,

As our way of congratulating you for finishing this book, and supporting you to grow your business and get your life back, we've created a unique online web tool kit to help you apply the ideas you've learned in this book.

To register, all you need to do is go online to **MauiMastermind.com/ freetoolkit** and gain immediate access to this powerful collection of business growth tools. It's designed to help business owners like you master the ideas in this book and build an owner-independent company.

Here's What You Get as Part of This Valuable *Free* Bonus:

- **Over a dozen video training modules** to help make building your business easier and faster.
- **Free PDF downloads** of many of the business growth tools David uses with his business coaching clients.
- **Free private 90-minute business coaching session** (if your business qualifies) to customize the strategies from the book to your specific situation so you can grow your company the right way.
- **And much more . . .**

You'll also Get 5 Complete Business "Short Courses" to Help You Blow Through Your Biggest Barriers to Growth

- The *"Grow Your Sales"* Short Course
  (6 Training Videos and PDF Action Guide)
- The *"Scale Your Operations"* Short Course
  (3 Training Videos and PDF Action Guide)
- The *"Financial Pillar"* Short Course
  (6 Training Videos and PDF Action Guide)
- The *"Strategic Planning"* Short Course
  (4 Training Videos and PDF Action Guide)
- The *"Time Mastery"* Short Course
  (3 Training Videos and PDF Action Guide)

Best of all, you'll be able to complete all these powerful training mini-courses from the comfort and convenience of your own home or office. You can watch them on your schedule.

How to Register for the Business Owner Tool Kit—FREE!

Simply go online to **www.MauiMastermind.com/freetoolkit** right now and complete the enrollment form. It's literally that easy.

Again, we thank you for reading this book. We wish you a lifetime of success and happiness. Enjoy your "graduation gift" of the *Business Owner Tool Kit!*

Sincerely,
David and Stephanie

P.S. Because this free tool kit is a limited time offer and may be changed or pulled at any time, we strongly encourage you to go to **www.MauiMastermind.com/freetoolkit** today and register. You'll kick yourself if you miss out.

A FINAL LETTER FROM DAVID FINKEL

Get Your Life Back Faster

Dear Reader,

Most business owners want growth, but they hold themselves back because they fear that to get that growth they'll have to sacrifice their lives. As you've learned in the 160 pages of this book, the only way to *sustainably* grow your company is to reduce its reliance on you, the owner. Done right, you get growth *and* you get your life back.

For over a decade now we've helped our business coaching clients build thriving owner-independent companies. On average, our clients enjoy an annual growth rate *five times higher* than the average privately held company in the United States while at the same time increasing their owner independence by 97.4 percent. And I wanted to invite you to explore the possibility of working together to help you scale your company and get your life back.

I do want to caution you: If you're looking for a magic bullet, the Business Coaching Program is not for you. It's for serious business owners who want to legitimately break through to the next level and build a thriving, owner-independent company.

Imagine tapping into this proven program. No more guessing; no more struggling; no more doubting yourself or your decisions. Just consistent growth and greater time freedom.

For years this is exactly what we've been doing—helping business owners just like you build a business, not a job.

And the most important thing of all is that we helped them do it by working *fewer hours.*

How can we be so confident that we can help you get great results? That's a fair question. And my answer is simple: We've done it ourselves—again and again.

Remember, our coaching team has built dozens of multimillion-dollar companies from the ground up. We've faced the same challenges you're facing: creating a winning business strategy, dealing with employee and vendor issues, controlling costs, and growing sales.

In fact, over the past 25 years, **the Maui coaches and advisors have personally scaled companies with an aggregate value of $63** *billion.*

But more important than the fact that we've done it in our own business lives is the impact our ideas and program have had on the lives of other business owners like you.

In the pages of this book you've already met *dozens* of our successful clients and learned about the dramatic difference working together has had on their businesses and their lives. What they all have in common is that they've recognized that being part of a *structured*, proven program is the fastest and surest way to succeed. And now it's your turn.

If you're serious about building an owner-independent business and want a structured, proven program to help you do it the best way possible, I urge you to go online to see if your business qualifies for a *free* one-to-one business coaching session. I'm not sure whether your business is a fit for the program, but I do know that there is only one way to find out— go to **www.MauiMastermind.com/freecoachingsession** right now.

If your business qualifies, we'll schedule a FREE 90-minute business coaching session focused on how to sustainably grow your company and get your life back. This private, one-to-one call is an actual *working session* on your business. We'll do a deep dive into your business and map out the best way to grow it. In fact, we'll do this session as if you were already one of our business coaching clients so that you can get a real sense of what it would be like to work with us, and we can get a real feel for what it would be like to work with you as a client if we invited you into the program.

There is no cost or obligation on either of our parts. Past experience has shown us that this is the most accurate way to try out the fit.

Either way, you'll leave the session with a greater sense of clarity about the best strategy to grow your company, including the top leverage points and concrete action steps to take.

Don't miss out on this opportunity. The Business Coaching Program was designed to give you the structure *and* the accountability, the map *and* the upgraded peer group, the direction *and* the feedback that you need to take your business to the next level.

You don't have to go it alone out there. Together, we will make certain that you'll succeed and reach your business goals.

Sincerely,

David Finkel
CEO
Maui Mastermind

P.S. Stop building your business in isolation and let our team coach and guide you. Go to **www.MauiMastermind.com/freecoachingsession** or call us toll-free at **1-866-737-9700** right *now*.

WHAT OUR CLIENTS SAY...

Tom Santilli
xByte, Inc.

"Before Maui I was successful (financially) with a business doing $5 million a year in sales with over $1 million in profit per year. But I was working myself to death to do it. I was working 80 hours a week and the stress was killing my health, my family, and just about everything else. Here I am seven years later and my company has **grown fourfold to over $20 million a year in sales, and over $3 million in profits**—and best of all, I'm literally not needed to do anything for the business anymore."

Jennifer Lyle
STS, Inc.

"The results speak for themselves: **Last year my business generated 9 times the operating profit.** I have more time off, am more relaxed, and have a much better quality of life. It's really hard to beat that return on my investment."

Paul Robinson
Ensunet

"Before Maui I was the typical lone-wolf business owner carrying everything on my shoulders. Now I have a peer group to challenge my thinking and push me to think bigger. **We've had 10x growth in the past 5 years in the program.**"

Andrea Butter
Patch of Shade

"Before I joined the Maui Mastermind Business Coaching Program, I worked 7 days a week, 10-12 hours a day. Since then, **my net profit has increased 10 times (1100%)**. More importantly to my quality of life and happiness, **I now only work about 20 hours a week**, and mostly on the kinds of work I really enjoy, such as designing new products. My contemporaries can't wait to retire from their jobs, but I can't imagine that for myself. My company brings me joy satisfaction, a purpose, and income – what's not to love?"

Dr. Shekhar Challa, MD
Kansas Medical Clinic

"**Our medical practice has been working with the Maui team now for roughly 36 months. Our top of line revenue increased by $4.1 million and our profits have grown too.** But the biggest impact from the program has been the growth in our leadership team as we've reduced our reliance on me and our practice COO. We have plans to continue to scale our multidisciplinary, state-wide practice further, and the business coaching program has been a valuable resource helping us to do it. I encourage any other medical group to get their help, both to grow your practice and to increase your personal time freedom."

Klayton Tapley
The Fireplace Place

"I got started with the Maui Mastermind Business Coaching Program four years ago. At the time I joined the program we were the typical owner-reliant business. We had sales of $700,000 and I was working 70 hours a week. Since then **we've scaled our sales to $3.5 million (350% increase)**. Best of all I've reduced my company's reliance on me and cut my working hours in half! I strongly recommend the program to any business owner who wants to both grow his company and gain more personal freedom."

Dr. Kimberly Nguyen
Cottage Dental

"**Over my last 12 months with the program my two dental offices have grown by 31% and 12% respectively.** What's more, my stress level has gone down tremendously and my team really understands where we want to go, and how building the practice to Level Three is good for their own job stability. I would recommend the program to any business owner who wants to build a business, not a job. The program gives you a step-by-step, cookbook approach of exactly how to grow and develop your business as a business."

RC Chavez
800-Buy-Kwik

"What's amazing to me is how quickly this has all happened. It's been less than a year in the program and my company is more profitable than ever. **We've driven our cost of capital down by half a million dollars or more, my team is fully on board in this process, and I have so much more time with my family.** What the program has shown me is that I could build the business to be more owner independent. I just needed a structured map and the accountability to do it differently. My only regret is that I didn't get started in the program sooner."

Mark Huha
Quality Property Maintenance, Inc.

"Over the past 36 months **we've doubled sales** and I've reduced my working hours from 70 hours per week down to 35. If you are serious about building a successful business, then my advice to you is to immediately get started working with the Maui team. It was one of the best business decisions I ever made."

Shirley Scholfield
Great Foundations Montessori

"I was working more than 14 hours per day, 7 days a week, and was literally overwhelmed by the business. If you had asked me before I started the Business Coaching Program if I could have ever let go of the feeling that I needed to personally perform or control every aspect of my business I would have told you no. What I realize now is that, while I am a great contributor to the business, if I build it all around me, I am its greatest limitation. Letting go hasn't been easy for me, but it has been so worthwhile. **I have more time for my family and have greatly reduced the stress in my life.**"

Brian Anderson
Hostek

"Ten years ago before joining the coaching program, life for me at my webhosting company, Hostek, was filled with 16-18 hour days, seven days a week. Vacation for me back then was taking my family to Busch Gardens for the day and working from a bench while my family rode the rides. I made the leap to join the program in 2012. Since that time, **the program helped me to 10x my company while at the same time reducing my work week to 20-25 hours a week.** One year ago I sold my company for a price that would have been unimaginable for me when I started this journey. I could not have done what I did without the Maui program and community."

Bonnie Hacker
Emerge

"Here I am six years after diligently applying these business strategies to build an owner-independent practice. **I've reduced my working hours to under 10 hours a week,** and the practice continues to serve the children we see exceptionally well. At the same time we've grown our revenues by 145% to $1,350,000 per year."

Dr. Gurpreet Padda
Surgeon and Entrepreneur

"I'm a surgeon with a thriving pain management and anti-aging practice. I'm also a serial entrepreneur with a dozen other businesses from restaurants, to medical billing services, to commercial real estate projects. The results speak for themselves—the program helped me to radically upgrade my use of time and make an **additional $1 million of net income**. I still use these same strategies and principles to this day and find them just as useful and profitable. **I don't see how any serious business owner can miss the opportunity to work with the Maui team and learn these and their other Level Three strategies.**"

Dr. Ken Le
PMR

"We've been scaling our rapidly growing medical systems which includes multiple clinics, surgery centers, and hospitals. Our Maui coach gives it to us straight and helps us focus on our highest leverage activities and opportunities. As a result, we've enjoyed tremendous growth and my team is fully engaged in this journey."

See if Your Business Qualifies for a FREE Business Coaching Session

Visit www.MauiMastermind.com/freecoachingsession
Or Call 1-866-737-9700 Right *Now*!
